Olé! Olé! Passion on a Plate

The Rise of Spanish Cuisine in London

To Sarah

from Cree.

Happy cooking!

Dec 2020

MILESTONE BOOKS

Greg Watts is an author and journalist. In his teens, he worked briefly in a fish and chip restaurant and as a kitchen porter in a hotel, experiences which he describes in his memoir, *The Long Road Out of Town*. When he's not writing, he enjoys cooking at his home in south-east London.

To Bea,
For all her encouragement
and brilliant ideas.

www.gregwattswriter.co.uk

ISBN:

978-0993188510

Published by Milestone Books, London

Printed and bound by Book Printing UK,
Remus House, Coltsfoot Drive,
Peterborough PE2 9BF

Contents

Acknowledgements

I must thank all those restaurant owners, chefs, and others involved in the Spanish hospitality industry in London for giving me their time and allowing me to peek into their fascinating world.

The suggestions and perceptive comments of my friend Saxon Bashford have been invaluable in getting me through periods when I was struggling with the book.

I would also like to thank Maggie Smith, Boris Rumney and Tom Thompson for their feedback and encouragement at the meetings of our Forest Hill writers' group

Thanks to copy editor Amy Bell, cover illustrator Lisa Maltby, and Silvia Porcu for her quirky map of London.

Finally, I would like to thank my wife, Bea, who has supported and encouraged me all the way throughout this project.

PRODUCTS FROM SPAIN

DON PEPE

THE HACIENDAS COMPANY

TAPAS REVOLUTION

ALBION WINES

DRAKE'S TABANCO

CAMINO

TOZINO

AMETSA WITH ARZAK INSTRUCTION

PIZARRO

CAMBIO DE TERCIO

MISS TAPAS

BRINDISA

 IN SEARCH OF

SPANISH FOOD AND WINE

I N   L O N D O N

1. Streets of Spain

I was sitting outside a small café in a street in Malaga, enjoying the early morning sunshine and the heat on my arms, and sipping my *café con leche*. The city was waking up under one of those crystal clear blue skies that are so common in the Mediterranean in August. From the main road that ran past the port, and along the coast to the resorts with their high-rise hotels and apartment blocks, I could hear the impatient pipping of car horns, the whining of mopeds, and the squeaking and roaring of buses filled with workers on their way to offices and shops. In the distance, a cruise ship sounded its horn.

Turning my head, I spotted an old man, dressed in a faded white T-shirt and tatty trousers and carrying a blue plastic bucket, ambling towards the café. He wandered up to the group of men in open-neck shirts and smart shoes at the table next to me, said something, and grinned. Then, plunging his hand into the bucket, he pulled out an octopus and raised it aloft. I watched, transfixed, as the helpless creature writhed, its tentacles making rapid movements like a snake. The old man dangled it in front of the men, water dripping onto the pavement. They stood up and gathered around it, like rugby players in a scrum. A discussion followed, with the old man shaking his head every so often and pointing excitedly to the octopus. *"¡Es grande! ¡Muy grande!"* he exclaimed. The waiter came out carrying a tray and joined in what was becoming the great octopus debate, forgetting about the customers waiting for their *churros*.

Eventually, a deal was struck. A bearded man with sunglasses pushed up on his head stubbed out his cigarette, pulled out a twenty euro note from his wallet and handed it to the old man, who stuffed it in his pocket and went on his way, waving over his shoulder. The bearded man then crossed the street, opened the boot of an Audi, and carefully placed the bucket inside before returning to join his friends.

Observing this curious episode persuaded me of the Spanish gift for understanding that the more local produce is, the fresher it will be. It also underlined how much the Spanish love anything caught in the sea. I couldn't imagine someone who had caught bream or eels in the Thames trying to sell them in the street in London.

The day before, with my wife, Bea, and five-year old son, Raphael, I had visited the Atarazanas indoor market in the centre of Malaga. Flags and paper lanterns hung across some of the streets, signalling that the week-long annual fair, a jamboree of fireworks, flamenco dancing and, of course, eating and drinking, was about to begin. The market building, with its stained glass depicting Malaga's history, slatted, Arab-style arch windows, and high glass and iron roof, was as impressive an example as you could find anywhere. The great horseshoe arch dates back to when Malaga was under Muslim rule and the site was a shipyard.

However, what made the visit unforgettable for me was not the architecture or the incredible array of produce – red and green peppers, tomatoes, artichokes, oranges and peaches, along with cheeses, spicy sausages, and meats. Instead, it was the fish and seafood I ate, wedged at the counter of a crowded booth. We must have spent an hour at that counter, nibbling on pieces of hake in batter, grilled tuna, and golden rings of *calamari*. I had never tasted seafood and fish so fresh and delicious. It was unbelievable. And it was made all the better by ice-cold bottles of Mahou beer.

"You know what?" I said to Bea, wiping my mouth with a paper napkin.

"What?" she asked.

"If I lived in Malaga, I'd be here every day."

Our friends Curro and Rebecca and their two-year old daughter were with us, having driven down from Zafra in Extremadura, a pretty town with a castle, bullring, and cosy bars, for a few days by the sea. Two years previously, Curro had given me a tour of his ham factory at Santa Olalla del Calla, a village on the border between Extremadura and Andalusia, in the foothills of the Sierra de Aracena mountains. As he took me around, he explained that many of the 15,000 hams hanging from the racks had been ordered by restaurants in Seville, which was why each one was dated: so he knew how long they had been cured for. But what struck me most about the factory was how spotlessly clean it was. I'd imagined blood-splattered walls and a terrible stench in the air.

Later on, I accompanied Curro to see some of his 2,500 black pigs a few miles outside the town. When he discovered that some of them had escaped into neighbouring fields, he immediately set off in pursuit. I stood there watching the comical scene as, shouting and waving a stick in the air, he chased the pigs back towards the gap in the fence they had wandered through. I wondered if I should be helping in some way, but I wouldn't have had a clue what to do, and besides, the pigs might have turned on me. Remarkably, he rounded them all up in just a few minutes.

It was an impressive sight, and one which helped me understand why the Spanish are so passionate not just about their fish and seafood but also about the ham produced by their black pigs. The experience was far removed from the first time I visited Spain. In 2005, I flew to Valladolid, a pleasant city in the Castilla y León region, with my eight-year old daughter, Suha, and booked into a small hotel in a narrow street near the main shopping area. Valladolid considers itself one of Spain's most important cities. It's where King Fernando and Queen

Isabel married in 1469, where Christopher Columbus died, and where Cervantes completed his masterpiece, *Don Quixote*. I didn't know any of this when I'd decided to go to Spain. I'd chosen Valladolid because a friend had gone there to train for the Catholic priesthood at its English College, an institution dating back to the Reformation. That was enough to make me feel a tenuous link with the city.

"Daddy, what do people in Spain eat?" Suha asked when we headed out in the sunshine to explore the city on the first morning.

"Er, different things", I said, as we waited to cross a busy street near the sixteenth-century cathedral.

"You mean pasta?" she asked.

"No, Italians eat pasta."

"What about burgers?"

"Well, probably not that much."

She frowned. "What do they like, Daddy?"

"Ah! *Paella*."

"What's *paella*?" she asked, as we turned into a narrow street with expensive-looking shops.

I explained that it was made with rice. Looking unimpressed, she asked me what else people in Spain ate.

"*Tortilla*", I said.

"What's that?"

"It's sometimes called a Spanish omelette."

"Ugh! I don't like omelettes."

The truth was that, apart from *paella* and *tortilla*, I didn't really know what kind of food people in Spain usually ate. I had a vague idea about it being "Mediterranean", but we were in north-west Spain, nearer to the Atlantic than the Mediterranean.

I recall little about the food in Valladolid, but I remember we seemed to spend a lot of time wandering the streets searching for a restaurant that included pizza or pasta on the menu. I didn't know what the Spanish dishes listed were, and anyway, I couldn't pronounce their names. In the mornings we would sit at a table outside a café in the vast Plaza Mayor, the city hall on one side festooned with flags, where we ordered croissants and orange juice. I'd never heard of *churros*, the fried tubes of pastry rolled in sugar and cinnamon which many Spaniards like to dip in hot chocolate for breakfast. When we took a coach one day in driving rain to the famous university city of Salamanca, we ended up eating fries and a kebab in a back street café, with a TV tuned to an Arabic channel and Spanish pop music blaring out. In fact, what I remember most about Valladolid is that, unusually, it had a beach beside the river where you could hire two-seater bikes and cycle merrily up and down the promenade.

It was a chef on TV who opened my eyes to Spanish food. It happened by chance when, at home one evening, I tuned into *Rick Stein's Spain* on BBC2. Listening to him enthuse about Spanish food and its relationship to the culture and turbulent but colourful history of Spain, I was captivated. He reminded me of my English teacher at college, who made literature come alive. I'd never realised food could be so interesting. And I underwent what you might call a culinary road to Damascus experience. It was one of those moments when you know something significant has changed inside you. Stein was presenting an image of food to me I had never seen before. It was intimately connected to the land and formed part of the identity of the people.

I grew up in a market town in the green hills of Derbyshire, but I felt no connection between what the local land produced and what we ate at home. When I looked out of the front window of the council house where we lived, I could see cows and sheep grazing in the distant fields, and often hear the chug of a tractor. If I went for a walk along the narrow lanes that led out of the town, I'd smell manure from the farms I'd pass, hear the sound of chickens clucking and pigs snorting, and see fields ripe with wheat and barley. The town had a butcher that sold the most amazing sausages, made with pork and sage, but, even though they were produced a few miles away and probably contained local ingredients, they were never marketed that way. They were just sausages. No one seemed bothered about the origin of what they were eating.

Apart from jars of homemade blackberry and gooseberry jam sold by smiling middle-aged ladies at the annual garden fête in the grounds of the Baptist manse, the only food whose origins I can remember knowing was fish. At the market on Tuesdays there would be a man in a white coat selling cod, smoked haddock, monkfish, and small tubs of prawns from a white trailer with the words "Grimsby Fish" painted on it. Yet the fishing port of Grimsby was about eighty miles away, so it could hardly be considered local.

There were two products Derbyshire was known for: the puddings (the locals, understandably, don't refer to them as tarts) made in Bakewell, the pretty town on the River Wye, and Stilton cheese made in a local dairy, but I don't recall a particular sense of local pride about either of them.

I've come to see that, while I grew up in the countryside, I also, paradoxically, grew up in an industrial area. Most of the people in the town worked in small textile mills, as I did immediately after leaving school, or in quarries, or drove the lorries that carted limestone all over the country. You would still see farmers in cloth caps standing around the bar of The Hope Anchor on market day, and each week the *Derby Evening Telegraph* would list the prices from the city's cattle market. But the world of farming seemed to have little to do with the rest of the local population.

My mum had grown up as one of six children, living in the middle of rural Ireland in the 1930s, when sprinkling sugar on a piece of bread was considered a treat. When we went on holiday to Ireland each summer, most meals consisted of things such as floury potatoes, bitter cabbage, pork chops, or steamed fish. The only meal I really enjoyed was the fry-up, which was always accompanied by white pudding, a kind of sausage made with oatmeal. Again, although the town was surrounded by farms, and straddled a river, the origin of the food was not considered important.

I have to say that my mum wasn't a great cook. I don't know if the nuns at her convent school taught her any culinary skills but, if they did, she didn't learn much. Even so, she was willing to try new things, unlike my dad, who was never happier than when eating a plate of baked beans on burnt toast, which was the only meal I remember seeing him cook. Maybe eating more exotic food was her way of trying to feel part of that glamorous world she saw in films and on TV, and which she read about in the women's magazines she used to buy, sitting up in bed and flicking through articles about clothes, how to be a good housewife, and new gadgets for the home. She knew that she could never really be part of it, working as a cleaner in a boarding school and living in a council house, but perhaps it made her feel connected to it. She could dream.

One day, she arrived home from the shops and plonked her blue shopping bag down on the living room table.

"What's for tea?" I asked as usual. I was always starving when I came home from school.

She pulled out a box and held it up. "This!"

"What's that?" I said, peering at the photo of yellow rice flecked with red and green.

"It's called *paella*. It's a new thing", she said, handing the box to me.

I examined it and saw that it showed a small map of Spain. All I knew about Spain was that it was famous for oranges, and that Leeds United under Don Revie had tried to summon some of Real Madrid's success by changing to an all-white kit.

Mum opened the box and there were two white sachets inside, one containing rice, the other a powdered mix with tiny pink prawns in it. After reading the instructions on the back of the box, she put a chunk of Kerrygold butter in the frying pan and, tipping in the rice, began to fry it. As the grains sizzled, they started to brown. She then gingerly poured in a jug of water and, checking the instructions again, turned up the gas flame to bring the pan to the boil. Finally, she shook in the colourful powder, lowered the gas, and left it all to simmer for twenty minutes.

When she put my plate in front of me and I took my first mouthful, I let out a long "mmm…" I'd never tasted anything like it before. I loved its creamy texture, the unfamiliar flavour, and the bite of the small prawns.

The fact that I can remember that *paella* all these years later tells me that it must have been a moment of some significance. Given that I was feeling trapped in a small town, perhaps the *paella* acted a signpost to a more exciting world.

Dining out in restaurants is something many of us now do regularly, not just on special occasions. For most working class families in Britain in the 1970s, eating out meant going to a fish and chip shop on a Saturday afternoon, or to a café serving beef and onion pie or, at the more daring ones, Chicken Kiev. Few pubs in those days served food. If you wanted something to eat, usually your only option was a bag of crisps or pork scratchings.

It wasn't until I was twenty-one that I went to what you would call a proper restaurant. Up until then, the nearest I'd come to this were occasional visits with my parents to Debenham's restaurant in Derby, and one occasion when we had a meal on the ferry from Liverpool to Dublin. Shortly before I left home to go to college in London, I took my mum to a pub in Derby that had a posh restaurant. It was a way of saying thank you to her and, perhaps, of marking a shift in our relationship. I was a young man now, not a boy. I can't remember what I ate, but I remember that she ordered salmon en croute. And I remember that when I left a tip after the meal I insisted to the waiter that whoever was washing the pots in the kitchen should receive it. At the time, my mum and I were working in the kitchen at a three-star hotel. She was a dish-washer and I was a kitchen porter. We knew just how hard you had to work to keep a kitchen clean and how little thanks you received for it. Being a dish-washer or a kitchen porter is still the lowest rung of the hotel ladder.

I don't recall many Spanish restaurants in London when I moved there in the 1980s. Back then, Spanish food had a poor reputation among the British. What attracted most of the millions of Brits flying out to Spain each summer were the beaches, sunshine, and cheap jugs of *sangria*. Many considered Spain to be like a Polo mint, which is to say that they didn't think there was anything interesting in the middle. When it came to food, most of those wandering between the restaurants on the Costas would opt for fish and chips, burgers, or hot dogs. I had done something similar when I had gone to Valladolid. Spanish food was thought to be all garlic and oil. "Foreign muck!" as my dad would have called it. By all accounts, those that did choose it from the menu were likely to be served defrosted *paella*, *gazpacho*, or other dishes that could be cooked in huge quantities.

The situation couldn't be more different today. Over the last decade or so it seems like new Spanish restaurants have been opening almost every month in London, especially in the West End and other areas that attract the more affluent, in search of fun and food. And, in most cases, the quality you will find is outstanding. The Soho tapas bar, Barrafina, came top in the 2015 National Restaurant Awards.

Just how popular Spanish food has become in London became apparent when I visited the Streets of Spain festival at the Southbank Centre with Bea and Raphael. When I first heard about the event, the name conjured up an image of a small, dark bar with a scuffed wooden floor and black and white photos on the wall. Laid out on the counter would be plates of red *chorizo* in wine and garlic, green *padrón* peppers, crispy rings of *calamari* with yellow *alioli*, and succulent meatballs in a rich tomato sauce. I imagined happy faces and bubbling chatter, as a barman in a short-sleeved white shirt served glasses of velvety Rioja wine and golden Estrella Damm beer.

When we arrived at the Queen Elizabeth Hall, though, it was heaving with people. We squeezed our way through the noisy crowds, the smell of chorizo and garlic filling the air, trying to work out what the different stalls were selling. With most it was hard to tell, because there were so many people gathered around, and everywhere you looked there were long queues. I peered curiously at the small paper plates everyone was clutching. People seemed happy to pay a fiver for what was really just a few mouthfuls.

It's not just Spanish food that has taken off. There's been an awakening of interest in Spanish wine, with critics going into raptures about it. For example, the international gastronomy magazine, *Der Feinschmecker*, named Raul Perez of Castilla y León its 2014 winemaker of the year. Rioja still dominates the shelves of UK supermarkets, although they are beginning to offer wines from other regions, such as Rías Baixas in Galicia and Jumilla in Murcia. In Spanish restaurants, however, you can taste wine from all over Spain, and diners are finding out that sherry is no longer just the stuff that Granny used to take as an occasional tipple.

The rest of the UK is far behind London when it comes to Spanish food, but this shouldn't come as a surprise, as London is now virtually a separate country. Still, you'll find Spanish restaurants in most large cities and even in some towns. And the London effect is rippling out. Iberica has opened restaurants in Leeds and Manchester, while Tapas Revolution has followed suit, opening up in Sheffield and Birmingham.

Supermarkets have been quick to respond to their customers' new interest in Spanish food, with many now stocking *chorizo*, Manchego cheese, Manzanilla olives, Ibérico ham, *tortilla*, and *pimentón*, along with ready meal *paella*. And, by all accounts, they are flying off the shelves.

Spain continues to be the top destination for British holiday-makers. As well as this, around 800,000 Brits have packed their bags and are living there permanently, and not all of them want apartments with swimming pools on the Costa Brava or Costa del Sol, English pubs with Sky TV, and shops that sell Heinz baked beans and custard creams. Thanks in part to various TV programmes, people are discovering that Spain isn't a polo mint after all, but a country of incredible landscapes, with romantic towns and villages built around ancient churches and castles, and of stylish and vibrant cities like Barcelona and Madrid. New motorways, the high-speed AVE trains, and budget airlines have all helped to make it much easier to explore the country.

At one time, when British people wanted to indulge their fantasies about living an idyllic life surrounded by olive trees and sunshine, they moved to Provence or Tuscany. Some now move to rural Spain. In his book, *Driving Over Lemons*, Chris Stewart describes how he and his wife sold their house in England and bought a run-down farm in the mountains surrounding Granada. Any romantic ideas they had quickly vanished, as they struggled to get to grips with a lack of electricity and fresh water, floods in the valley, and being accepted by the locals. If I were ever to move to Spain, then it would have to be to a town. I don't think I could hack it living in the mountains. I like my creature comforts too much.

Catholicism might have lost much of its influence in Spain, but its holy days and saints' days are still enthusiastically celebrated. People dress up in medieval costumes, and wobbling statues of the Virgin Mary or Christ are carried solemnly on men's shoulders through crowded streets. It goes without saying that lots of eating and drinking takes place, and that there's music and dancing into the night.

Every year, too, thousands of people set off on the route of Santiago de Compostela in Galicia, in whose cathedral the bones of the apostle St James are said to be kept. I suspect that most of those who hitch on a backpack and set off on these winding roads, their signposts decorated with scallop shells, are not doing this for religious reasons. This is a new kind of pilgrimage, more about finding yourself than finding God.

The Spanish have a much stronger sense of regional differences than the British. Spain is made up of seventeen regions, and everyone insists their produce is the best, which explains why there are so many festivals each year celebrating it. For example, in Cuenca in Castilla-La Mancha they honour garlic, in Trujillo in Extremadura they venerate cheese, and in Gijón in Asturias it's cider. *Paella* could arguably be described as Spain's national dish, and with its red and yellow it even resembles the flag. Valencia is Spain's rice growing region, and in the town of Sueca they hold an international *paella* competition, where chefs cook the dish over burning wood in huge pans. At Pontes in Galicia, they celebrate a green vegetable called *grelo*, although the town ended up marketing an entirely different festival in 2015 when it used Google to translate this Galician word into Castilian – people were mistakenly invited to take part in a "clitoris festival".

Of course, you can't talk about Spain without talking about tapas, and more and more visitors to Spain have been won over by this tradition of serving small dishes of food. It's not uncommon today to hear Londoners talk about going for tapas, in the same way they talk about going for an Indian or a pizza. Sharing small dishes with your dining partner rather than ordering your own is a novel way of eating if you are used to a starter, main, and dessert. And these smaller portions are particularly appealing to those who are calorie-conscious and who have an eye on utilising their gym membership.

There are different stories about the origins of tapas, a word which derives from *tapar*, the Spanish verb "to cover", and everyone you talk to has their favourite. One theory is that it goes back to when pieces of ham or cheese were placed over the top of a drink to keep the flies away. Some say that tapas began when King Felipe III became alarmed by widespread drunkenness and ordered that bars should place a small amount of food over the mug or goblet to slow the effects of alcohol. Others believe that tapas originated when the thirteenth-century king Alfonso X of Castilla became very ill and was permitted to eat only small bites of food and a little red wine. After he had recovered, he ordered that wine not be served unless it was accompanied by a small snack.

It's traditional when you go out for an evening in Spanish towns and cities to move from one tapas bar to another, having a drink and a small dish of something at each one. Tapas bars often specialise in certain dishes. One might be known for seafood and fish, another for meat. This is the Spanish answer to the British pub crawl, which was treated like an Olympic sport when I was growing up. The Spanish might enjoy running with the bulls, and they might be noisy at times, but they don't usually get into fights at closing time or start smashing things up, like you see in the streets of many British cities at weekends. The Spanish go out to drink and eat, while the British go out to drink or eat. In Britain someone will usually say "Let's go to the pub" or "Let's go for a meal". In Spain, people will say "Let's go for tapas".

In Granada, the Andalusian city overlooked by the amazing Alhambra palace, the council has designated a street in the centre as the "Tapas Trail". What's brilliant about Granada is that every time you order a drink in a bar or restaurant it comes with a small plate of something, such as olives, a slice of tortilla, or a couple of ham croquettes. What an incredibly cheap way to eat, I thought, the first time this happened. Then, after visiting several bars, I began to feel a little guilty for not paying anything.

"When I was in Seville, you didn't get free tapas in the bars", I remarked to a waiter.

Smiling, he replied "this only happens in Granada." The way he said it indicated that he was proud that his city maintained this wonderful tradition.

Spanish food is not all about tradition, though. Chefs such as Juan Mari Arzak in the Basque Country and Ferran Adrià in Catalonia, with their modern and imaginative approaches to preparing and cooking ingredients, have become culinary superstars.

Adrià's restaurant, elBulli, located near the coastal town of Roses, scooped three Michelin stars, becoming a kind of shrine or, if you prefer, Euro Disney of gastronomy. Pilgrims descended on it, hoping for culinary ecstasy and maybe a glimpse of the saviour. According to The New York Times, 300,000 people tried to book in one year. Given that the restaurant had only fifteen tables, most were disappointed. Those who did secure a table might have worked their way through a thirty-dish tasting menu, including frozen coconut milk with curry powder, baby cuttlefish with pesto ravioli, a single strawberry grilled with gin and juniper, or mango and begonia flower tea. When it came to food, it seemed the only thing Adrià couldn't do was multiply loaves and fishes.

Adrià has documented and photographed every dish he created. They appear in the restaurant's *General Catalogue*, which, as described by Coleman Andrews in his biography of Adrià, runs to over 2,400 pages. Adrià has also produced *A Day at elBulli*, subtitled "An insight into the ideas, methods and creativity of Ferran Adrià". Its 600 pages include photos not just of the food but of the people producing it and all aspects of the restaurant. If Adrià is a culinary messiah, then these books could be likened to culinary Old and New Testaments.

Adrià is a fascinating character and someone whose influence on cooking has been felt beyond Spanish cuisine. I remember watching a YouTube clip of him standing on a stage at the Culinary Institute of America in New York and demonstrating some of his techniques to a hall packed with young chefs. It looked more like a magic show than a cookery demonstration. "It's not so hard to be a good chef", Adrià had told them through an interpreter. "It's a matter of practice and affection." He had spoken about creating a "new culinary language" and had said that gastronomy should be about pleasure. The students had watched him make tagliatelle out of mango and, using an electric hand mixer, a foam out of carrot juice. It was then time for his party piece: spherification, which he has become famous for. One of his assistants had mixed yoghurt with water in a glass, then placed a spoon of it into a mixture of alginate – a natural gelling agent produced from brown seaweed – and water. As if by magic, the blob of yoghurt solidified, while remaining liquid inside. Pleased with the reaction of his audience, Adrià had gone on to show how food products once considered waste could be transformed. A cauliflower could be used as a substitute for couscous by removing the small seeds, placing them in a blender to create a powder, and then blanching them in boiling water.

Likewise, the seeds of a tomato shouldn't be thrown away but used to make a gelatine. These seem such simple ideas but, apparently, no one had thought of them before. A key idea in Adrià's philosophy is that cooks need to be creative, and creativity means not copying anyone else.

Nevertheless, not all Spanish chefs became disciples of Adrià. The late Santi Santamaria, whose restaurant El Racó de Can Fabes, located in a farmhouse in the hills north of Barcelona, became the first Catalan restaurant to be awarded three Michelin stars, dismissed Adrià's cooking as pretentious and argued that using things such as liquid nitrogen with food could be harmful. He advocated using seasonal ingredients and cooking in the traditional Catalan way.

Arguably, Spain has now taken France's crown as the gastronomic king of Europe. In the nineteenth century a French writer remarked that Spain had thousands of priests but not a single cook. No one would ever suggest that now. The wonderful Keith Floyd talked about how wars and invaders, especially the Moors, shaped it into one of the most culturally and gastronomically rich countries of the world. "Add to that the influences that resulted from the discovery of the Americas and you have a glorious bubbling pot of flavours, tastes and textures", he said.

The arrival of so many Spanish restaurants in London is part of this picture, but can also be seen as only one feature of the city's booming restaurant scene. I don't know if London has the best cuisine in the world, but I do know that if you decide to go out for a meal, you are spoilt for choice. The types of cuisine on offer and the number of restaurants is staggering. According to a 2014 report from *The Caterer*, London boasts around 6,500 restaurants.

The word restaurant comes from the French verb "to restore", and it seems that many of us feel we need a lot of restoring in our daily lives. *Harden's* annual guide to London's restaurants provides an accurate picture. Its 2015 edition recorded 148 new restaurants opening against 47 closures. In the 2016 edition the number opening had shot up to 179 against 56 closures. The guide's co-founder Peter Harden remarked, "The growth of the London restaurant scene is jaw-dropping in comparison to its recent past, never mind the dark ages in which we founded our guide twenty-five years ago."

This restaurant boom reflects how dramatically eating habits in Britain have changed in the last thirty or so years. For a long time, Britain had a dismal reputation when it came to food. Perhaps this had something to do with the rationing introduced by the government from the Second World War to 1954. Most working class families learned to live frugally and make do. Food was just fuel to keep you going.

When I was a child, most of what I ate at home came out of a tin or a frozen packet. If you looked in the kitchen cupboards of many working class families in Britain in the 1970s you would see the same things: tins of Heinz baked beans and spaghetti, minced beef, corned beef, luncheon meat, garden peas, sardines, pilchards (for the cats), John West salmon, and Fray Bentos steak and kidney pie. The fridge would be stocked with Findus fish fingers, Birds Eye cod in parsley sauce, beef burgers, and the dreaded Walls skinless sausages. As for adding flavour to food, out would come the bottles of HP Sauce, tomato ketchup, or Worcestershire Sauce. The novel culinary ideas of the food writer, Elizabeth David, hadn't yet spread to small market towns in Derbyshire.

Since those days, there has been a huge shift in attitudes to food and eating out. We use terms such as "organic", "sustainable", and "free range" to talk about produce, even if we aren't always sure exactly what they mean. And because we are supposed to be more aware of health and the environment, the labels and packaging tell us about our food's origins, ingredients, and methods of production. But who really understands them? With some labels, you need a PhD in chemistry to make any sense of the information.

Terms like "vindaloo", "dim sum", "sushi", "taco", and "meze" are now part of our culinary vocabulary. In London you can eat food from virtually any country in the world. And you no longer have to go into the West End to do this. For example, in Crystal Palace, up the road from where I live, the amazing variety of restaurants is typical of many areas of the capital. You have Japanese, Venezuelan, Portuguese, Vietnamese, Iranian, Brazilian, and French/Algerian, not to mention the usual Indian, Chinese, and Italian establishments, and several gastropubs. I'm sure it won't be long before a Spanish restaurant opens there. Today, you no longer have to book a flight to see the world; you can see it on a plate in your local restaurant.

Food is no longer just about eating, as it was in my childhood. It's spawned its own sub-culture, with umpteen TV programmes devoted to it, as well as whole sections in newspapers and magazines, blogs, web sites with hundreds of recipes, and numerous awards each year. And as well as all this, we have farmers' markets, cookery schools and classes, private chefs, pop-up restaurants, "underground" restaurants, and food festivals like Streets of Spain.

In part, all of this has been brought about by countless TV chefs who come into our homes, do their magic and then persuade us to buy their cook books. If you go into any charity shop today, the chances are that the largest section of books will be those devoted to cookery and eating – and the next largest section will be books about going on a diet. Every year more and more cookery books are churned out, yet chilled ready meals and takeaways are as popular as ever. We like to watch other people cook. Cooking has become entertainment, the kitchen a theatre, and chefs have become actors.

What, then, is the story behind this recent rise of Spanish cuisine in London? What is the essence of Spanish food? What makes it distinctive, and is it, as some suggest, the new Italian? As with anything new, it is individuals who are driving progress. I was curious about the key personalities responsible for this change to the gastronomic map of London, and the chefs who have left Spain to come and make their mark in our capital. I had no idea, for instance, how easy it was to turn a passion into a successful business.

So I decided to set out on the streets of London on the trail of Spanish food. I'd hardly ever written about food before in my career as an author and journalist. And my experience in the food and hospitality industry was limited to my time as a teenage kitchen porter, a brief stint behind the counter of a fish and chip shop, and, when I first came to London, a job pulling pints in a rough south London pub.

I suspected that this would be an advantage rather than a disadvantage. I wouldn't be approaching the subject as a clever clogs food writer who has seen it all, but as someone curious to understand what has to be the most remarkable culinary phenomenon to hit London in a long time.

I was going to embark on a journey around Spain, like Rick Stein had done in his BBC series, except that in my case I wasn't going to leave London.

2. The Revolutionary

"I wanted to show that it's possible for anyone to cook great Spanish food, whether you are a single mum with a child or a group of students, with what you can find in your local supermarket or shop."

Omar Allibhoy, Tapas Revolution

Knowing of my love for Spanish food, for Christmas Bea bought me a gift voucher for a tapas class at Leith's School of Food and Wine, situated in a small street between Shepherd's Bush and Acton. I arrived there one morning in February and took my seat in the demonstration kitchen with about thirty other keen home cooks, all of us hoping to improve our knowledge and techniques. A guy with long black hair and a beard breezed in and, grinning, introduced himself as Omar Allibhoy before proceeding to give us a potted biography of his life. As I listened to him, I wondered why he was going on like this instead of getting straight down to the cooking. I'd attended two other classes at Leith's and neither of the chefs had thought it necessary to go into this much detail about their careers. After Omar had finished his introduction, he speedily and expertly demonstrated how to cook clams with Serrano ham and *fino* sherry, then dished it up and passed plates around for each of us.

"So, why have you chosen a tapas class?" he asked, moving between the rows of chairs.

"Because of your book", a young woman piped up excitedly.

Several other students nodded in agreement, and Omar looked pleased. I had no idea he had written a popular book, and now felt foolish for my earlier reaction. When we went upstairs to the kitchen for the class, a pile of copies of *Tapas Revolution* lay on a work surface by the door.

A few months later, I came out of Shoreditch High Street Station and made my way towards Tapas Revolution on Bethnal Green Road. As I turned a corner, I spotted Omar, dressed in his black chef's jacket and black jeans, bending down to tidy up some boxes of plants on the pavement outside the bar. Checking my watch, I realised I was twenty minutes early, so I decided to go for a wander.

When I first got to know Shoreditch in the 1980s, it was a shabby area sitting awkwardly between the City and the East End, full of small clothing companies, warehouses, spit and sawdust pubs, and scruffy looking cafés. Now it's at the heart of London's media, art, and technology industries and, like its neighbour Hoxton, has become a byword for cool. At one time, tourists never ventured this far. Today they come to take photos and wander up and down the streets. A shop called Shoreditch Junk, in a run-down building attached to one of the arches of the derelict railway viaduct, has a sign in the window saying "Kiss my black ass" and, for some reason, a statue of the Virgin Mary next to it. Neighbouring lock-ups have been spray-painted in garish colours in the kind of graffiti some people like to call art.

This dramatic change in Shoreditch, helped by it becoming connected to the Overground railway network, is reflected in the food now on offer. On the short walk from the station to Tapas Revolution I passed stalls selling "chunky Buddha tacos", Brazilian *churros*, Peruvian-style grilled chicken, and Greek street food. Also close to Tapas Revolution are branches of Byron and Wasabi, and an Italian deli.

Even so, there were reminders of the old Shoreditch. Gina's restaurant was still there, although I wasn't sure if it was open for business, as the "G" in the sign had dropped off and the phone number still contained the 071 prefix, which was replaced in 1995. However, at the top of Brick Lane, where most of the shops have the word "vintage" in the name and hipsters stand behind the counters of the coffee shops, the two twenty-four-hour bagel shops, a long-time favourite of black cab drivers, were still doing a brisk trade, offering salmon and cream cheese bagels at £1.60 and chopped herring bagels at £1.

I wondered how much longer the bagel shops would last. Diggers were clawing at the earth on a piece of empty land with hoardings proclaiming Galliard Homes, one of the large property developers gobbling up chunks of London at an incredible rate and building blocks of monotone flats that few people can afford to buy. Many of these properties are marketed as investments for the rich in the Middle and Far East rather than as homes for Londoners. No doubt these flats will look identical to the ones across the road, and be even more expensive.

I walked back to Tapas Revolution and introduced myself to a waiter, who motioned me to a seat by the window, saying Omar would be with me shortly. While I was waiting, I took the opportunity to examine the decor. It was bright and cheerful with lots of grey, white, black, and brown, in what you might call a contemporary minimalist style. The ceiling was made from unvarnished planks of wood, and stools hung upside down in one of the large windows. Pots of basil stood on the horseshoe-shaped bar with its blue, white, and salmon-coloured Estrella beer pumps. Behind it were oranges in baskets and rings of *chorizo* hanging from coat hooks. It was clearly designed for trendy diners.

When Omar joined me at the table, I was immediately struck by the energy he exuded. This was even more remarkable given that the day before, he had caught an early morning train to Birmingham for a meeting and, in the evening, had taught a class at Leith's, not finishing until 10.30 pm. I guessed that he had been hard at it in the kitchen at

Tapas Revolution since early morning. I began by asking him why he thought tapas had become so popular in London.

"You know, everyone wants to do tapas now", he said. "One out of two restaurants opening in London has small plates. Chinese tapas, Italian tapas, Indian tapas, French tapas. No matter where you go, that is the trend."

So what's behind it all?

"It's about sharing. When you share food it connects. I think the world needs a lot of connection. That's why tapas has become big. It's no longer about small plates of Spanish food. It's about small plates of food. People want this everywhere. You share your stories, you share your life. But it always starts in the *calle*, the street. The name of the company that owns this restaurant is Ibericos Etc (Calle). We want to bring that communal aspect of Spain to people. We want people to talk to each other, to share their stories even if they don't know each other."

I hadn't expected such a philosophical explanation of tapas, but the Spanish have a different understanding about food and life than the British. Omar smiled when I mentioned my wife's belief that Spaniards like to be in groups. "If you ask a British person what comes to mind when someone says home, the answer I normally get is that people think about physicality: their house, the decoration, my space. If you ask someone Spanish the same question they will say my family and my friends. The last thing they will think of is the physicality of the place they live in. For most of the year the weather is good in Spain and when the weather is good you spend more time out in the streets, in the communal places, in the terraces, in the squares, walking by the beach, not in the private places. Private places are seen as restraining you from other people."

Many of us Brits would really like to be Spanish, Omar thinks. Spain is where we go on holiday (fifteen million of us in 2015) and where many of us dream of retiring to. All the same, for some Brits who go to Spain, he acknowledged, the local food isn't always an attraction. "There is something we do wrong in Spain. We believe we need to give you what you want and what you are used to as opposed to what we do well. We should give you what we do well because when you have our deep fried squid, our prawns, our *chorizo*, you love it."

Over the centuries Spain too has absorbed influences in food from other cultures, Omar explained. For example, learning from the Arabs how to cultivate olive trees and produce the oil, and from the Italians how to salt sardines. And much of the cod eaten in Spain has traditionally been caught in the waters of northern Europe. Yet when it comes to being adventurous with food, Spain is a long way behind Britain, he maintained. "In Spain up until ten years ago no one knew what sushi was. And still a lot of people don't know what it is. Spain has remained very Spanish until today. It's only in the last ten years that our supermarkets have started looking more like yours."

Tapas Revolution on Bethnal Green Road had been open only a few weeks and was Omar's latest branch, following those at the Westfield shopping centre in Shepherd's Bush and the Bluewater shopping centre near Dartford in north Kent. Running a restaurant in Shoreditch is very different from running a restaurant in Westfield or Bluewater, he has realised. Whereas many of those who shop at Westfield have a high disposable income and are well travelled, at Bluewater people are much more money-conscious and many would rather go to La Tasca, because it is cheaper. Two tapas bars in a shopping centre is one too many, he has concluded.

Opening at Westfield was a difficult decision for him to make, he revealed. "I had very high standards and wondered if by going into a shopping centre I might destroy my reputation. It seemed very dangerous. But I also saw it as a fantastic opportunity. I wanted to stop cooking food with those modernist techniques and provide real Spanish tapas." Although his Bethnal Green Road restaurant is on the edge of the City, most of his clientele don't work in banks or insurance companies but are young professionals who have moved into the area, or are working in the small creative companies in the surrounding streets.

Omar is just as passionate about the look of his restaurants as he is about the taste of the food he serves. He has paid attention to the smallest details, believing that if you get the small things right, you will get the big things right. The ceramic beer pumps are handmade in Galicia, the lamp shades are made from fishing nets from Catalonia, and the white salt and pepper pots come from Almería in Andalusia, famous for providing the locations for Sergio Leone's Spaghetti Westerns, as well as for *Lawrence of Arabia* and *Indiana Jones*. Omar has even designed the staff uniforms.

"I'm a restaurateur. I'm not just a chef. I like doing what nobody does", he said, showing me a handmade plate which had been pressed and glazed with the pattern of an old Spanish curtain. "I'm a bit of a restaurant freak, but I think all these things make a difference." When I asked why there are no pictures on the wall, he answered that he is planning to put some up, probably colourful frames with black and white photos inside, what he calls "old fashioned retro with a bit of modern".

Omar arrived in London nine years ago to begin his revolution. He was born in the centre of old Madrid and lived there until he was four, before moving to a suburb in the north of the city. His family comes from Cava Baja, a street famous for its tapas bars. "There is a tapas bar now where they lived", he noted approvingly. His entrepreneurial spirit may have something to do with his father, who was born in India and worked in the coffee business for thirty years, buying land and growing coffee in South America. But it was Omar's mother who sowed the seeds of his future culinary career. "The first memory of my life is of my mum cooking. I would have been about two. It was a flan and I remember very vividly sitting on the floor a couple of metres away from the burners and the oven. I remember my mum making the caramel, putting the contents into the mould and putting it into the oven, and the aromas. I also remember drinking the milkshakes my mum made with orange, banana, biscuits, and milk and blended all together. When I had one of those, I was in heaven. And it was from this that I began a love affair with food."

He began helping his mum in the kitchen, whisking eggs and baking, but soon became bored with her dishes and started to experiment. "After coming home from school and playing football for the local team, I would prepare dinner. This was my hobby – it was my game. Then suddenly I said, this is what I want to do for the rest of my life." His mum baked well, but she didn't cook that well, he maintained. "I became the head chef of the house when I was eight years old. She also called me the kid of the spices, because I put spices into everything. I would make a Bolognese sauce and put curry powder in it."

The cook book an aunty gave him when he was six was one of those pivotal moments we all have in childhood. "I used to also cook with her because she took care of me when I was little and both my parents were at work. It was called *My First Cookery Book*, and I still have it at home. I cooked all the recipes in it. They were very simple and came with drawings. If it said use three oranges, there would be drawings of three oranges. One recipe was a pizza made with a slice of English bread with *passata* and cheese on top, which you put in the oven. This was an important cook book for me, probably the most important cook book of my life."

During the long school holidays he would spend much of the time in the kitchen, but his mother told him off for cooking too much food that went to waste. So he began selling cakes, tarts, and waffles in the back garden. His family members, especially his brother, were his fiercest critics. However, "If there was one dish the family praised, it was a cheesecake with quince pastry. They loved it and I made it as a Christmas dessert for a few years."

When he went to secondary school he displayed little interest in the classroom and found it difficult to summon the motivation to complete his homework. By now, he was dreaming of becoming a chef and at thirteen began attending a cookery school in the evenings. "When I finished at the cookery school I decided that I wanted to start working and didn't want to study any more. Nor did I want to study hospitality or culinary arts. I just wanted to cook. My parents said, 'What if one day you change your mind and don't want to be a chef? You won't be able to go to university if you don't go to high school. Don't put that barrier in your life.' So I completed my high school studies."

As he was talking, a man in a white coat arrived pushing a trolley stacked with boxes of cod from Billingsgate Market, and Omar leapt up to inspect them. "Smell how fresh the fish is. It's amazing!" Omar enthused, tearing open a box.

His first job in catering was as a kitchen porter at a Madrid pizza restaurant, where the chef promised to teach him how to cook after he had finished cleaning. "It was a brilliant kitchen. They were very well organised. I learned how to make pizzas and everything. But it was the organisation that struck me. It's one thing to cook at home, but another thing to cook in a professional kitchen. It was the first time I had been in one and I found it fascinating. I paid a lot of attention to what was going on."

After a year, he got a job at the five-star InterContinental Hotel, which served Spanish and French cuisine, and then at a new Madrid restaurant called Nhube, at that time run by Ferran Adrià.

"Adrià said, 'If we take you on, you will have to cut your hair,'" Omar recalled. "And I had long hair, very long hair. I said, 'No problem – I'll cut it tonight.' He said, 'OK, the job is yours. And you don't have to cut your hair.'"

After three years, Omar was promoted to sous chef and went on to work in two other Adrià restaurants. However, he wanted to expand his horizons and learn about other cuisines. He also wanted to learn English and toyed with the idea of travelling to India or Thailand, but in the end flew to Canada, where he was kicked out after a month for breaching immigration rules.

Like Jesus preparing for his ministry, Omar then embarked on a forty-day gastronomic tour around Spain with three friends. In July 2005 he was in Pamplona, to see the running of the bulls, when he saw on TV that there had been a terrorist attack in London. The carnage struck a particular chord with him, as the woman who cleaned his parents' home had been injured in the Madrid train bombings the year before. He had been contemplating setting off again, maybe to the US, Australia, or South Africa, but instead something told him to board a flight to London.

He moved into a flat around the corner from Tapas Revolution's present site in Shoreditch, printed seventy copies of his CV, and began visiting high end restaurants and five-star hotels in search of a job. "I thought I would have a better chance in a hotel because the teams in the kitchen are really big and I couldn't speak English. Communication in a kitchen is vital. You have to be able to follow a service and understand what you are being asked to do."

Impressed by his time under Ferran Adrià, a hotel in Covent Garden took him on. "They put me in the kitchen restaurant, but I couldn't understand what people were telling me or asking me to do. After one evening they moved me to breakfast and banqueting, because it was easier."

He knew that Marco Pierre White and Gordon Ramsay had blazed a trail in the kitchens in London and he wanted a piece of the action. He did stints at Picasso in Greek Street, owned by White, and the Michelin-star Maze, owned by Ramsay ("fierce but very interesting") and where Jason Atherton, another rising star, was head chef.

Omar wasn't impressed by the tapas dishes Maze was serving. He thought they were too complicated. "I always told them this is not tapas. Tapas is made to be shared. What was being served were just small plates of beautiful food. And that's not the same. Tapas is more than just the food. It's the way you enjoy it. It was at this time that I started to realise how little Spanish food there was in London and the UK. There were very few Spanish restaurants. I thought, maybe there's an opportunity here."

He uploaded his CV to Caterer.com and soon received a call from a Spanish restaurant called Essence, whose head chef, Nieves Barragán Mohacho, was leaving to work in a new restaurant called Fino, which went on to win praise from food critics. "I joined the kitchen and did really well for them for about a year. They were very impressed by my techniques, because Nieves was very traditional and I was the opposite. I was very modern and creative."

When he mentioned that he met his sous chef Danny there, who became his best friend, I said that Anthony Bourdain in *Kitchen Confidential* likens a chef's relationship with a good sous chef to that of a married couple. "You know, I call Danny 'darling' in Spanish", he said, giving a chuckle.

The desire began to grow in him to set up his own restaurant. Having worked for some of the biggest names in the culinary world, he felt he was ready for the challenge. When he noticed that some of the pubs he visited used their kitchens only for storage, he spotted an opportunity. "I loved pubs. Every time I met someone we would go to the pub. I thought it was the closest thing to a tapas bar. But I felt pubs could improve if they served tapas. So I thought what if we start running these kitchens. So I quit my job and began knocking on doors."

The owner of the Grave Maurice on Whitechapel Road was intrigued by the brash Spaniard who turned up at his door. "I said to him I would buy the crockery, buy the cutlery, fix the equipment if it's broken, hire the chefs, take care of health and safety. All you have to do for us is to set the tables and take the money. He said, 'Let's give it a try.' And that's what we did. The first thing we had to do was clean the kitchen. I'd never seen dust so thick. It had built up over years and years. The kitchen had a grill, burners, *plancha*, fryers, freezers, fridges, everything you can imagine."

Omar began offering tapas and *paella*, but because he didn't have any PR, it took a while to catch on. "People loved being able to have a nibble while having a pint. Some people would eat it at the bar, others sitting down having a meal."

Buoyed by his success, he did the same at the nearby Blind Beggar, remembering how his father had talked about the advantages of replicating business models. I was surprised by this. When I had last been there, for the relaunch of a book I'd written with a former East End gangster, it had seemed like the kind of place where someone was more likely to put a glass in your face than a bowl of tapas in front of you. It seemed pretty much the same kind of pub as it was when the notorious Kray brothers used to frequent it in the Sixties. This was another example of how the eating and drinking landscape in London had changed so dramatically in just a few years.

Omar then took his tapas concept to Studio 54 in Vauxhall, The Harwood Arms and The Malt House in Fulham, and a bar in Battersea. It seemed he was on a roll and nothing could stop him.

However, it all came crashing down following the introduction of the smoking ban in 2007 and the economic crisis that broke out in 2008. "At that point I literally lost everything I had. I was in debt. I owed money to suppliers. I owed money to the bank, to my parents. So I asked myself what do I do. The disappointment of failure was immense, but I was only twenty-five and I knew I needed to start again. I'm not a person who works well for others. I need to be my own boss because I have a particular way of doing things."

Realising that he would have to work for someone else now, he went to a firm of head-hunters and asked if they knew of anyone opening a new Spanish restaurant who might be interested in him. He eventually got taken on at El Pirata de Tapas in Westbourne Grove, Bayswater. It had been open only two months, but the owner wasn't happy with the head chef and there were problems in the kitchen.

"I said I'm a good chef and I can do good things for you but I'm looking for someone to back me in the future. He agreed. Two years later we were in *MasterChef*, doing well in big competitions and listed as one of the best restaurants in the UK. The restaurant was an incredible success and made loads of money. There were a lot of tapas bars in London, but no one was cooking the kind of food I was. There were good tapas bars, such as Fino, Barrafina, and Brindisa, but they weren't doing what we were doing. I produced a lot of molecular cuisine using techniques I'd learned in Spain. It was a time when Londoners were looking for creativity and innovation in their meals. People were going to restaurants not just for the food but to have a good time with the food as well."

Dismayed at how little most English people seemed to know about Spanish food, Omar took to the road in 2010 to preach the gospel of tapas. When he had worked in pubs he had seen many people getting drunk because they were not eating. Tapas, he believed, could improve people's behaviour. It wasn't just about food, it was also about morality. At the same time, he also wanted to "create some noise" and raise his own profile. "One day I was looking at the map of England and wondering where I should go and I took a pen and wrote a T, which went from the west to the east coast and all the way down to the Isle of Wight. And I thought what if I follow this T and I just cook with anyone I find along the way."

So, on his days off from El Pirata, he headed out of London with a simple message: repent and eat tapas. He cooked in market places, homes, parks, gardens, and even while punting on the river in Oxford. He took over a fish and chip shop in Grimsby for a morning, replacing ketchup with *alioli* and the fish and chips with a type of shark, marinated and deep fried, and *patatas bravas*. In a pub in Nuneaton he provided free tapas with every beer.

"What people want to do is relax and chat", he said, leaning back in his chair to make his point. "I wanted to show that it's possible for anyone to cook great Spanish food, whether you are a single mum with a child or a group of students, with what you can find in your local supermarket or shop."

After the owner of El Pirata agreed to back him in a restaurant venture, he considered establishing the kind of restaurant that might win a Michelin star, but in the end decided to take a more commercial route. And Tapas Revolution was born.

Like many modern restaurants, Tapas Revolution has open kitchens. To my mind, this is one of the most welcome recent developments. If you can see what the chefs are doing, there's less chance they might do the kind of things you suspect sometimes happen in kitchens. But Omar has gone one step further in having the chefs serve customers their food. "This is something particular to us. I like this connection.

I'm also a chef, and when I was at El Pirata de Tapas I was always going to the floor to ask customers how their meal was. I found it really gratifying when they told me it was delicious. But it's not the same when customers pass you a message through a waiter. Or if you received criticism from a customer, you would take it more personally and it would drive you. Also, instead of the food standing there and getting cold for a while, any of the chefs can pick it up, take it to a table, give a nice smile and go back to the kitchen. Sometimes he might need to take some plates back with him and give them to the kitchen porter."

Omar signalled to a waiter for some tapas and asked me if I would like to join him. That was an easy one to answer. He called out to one of the staff and, within minutes, small dishes started landing on the table: *patatas bravas*, broken eggs with baby eels, octopus, and *croquetas de jamón*.

"Did you like the pork cheeks?" he asked.

"Delicious", I said. "What was the sauce?"

"Chocolate."

"Chocolate!"

I'd seen savoury dishes cooked with sweet things on *Saturday Kitchen* on TV, but the idea had never appealed to me. I couldn't see how this would work. But the incredibly soft, melt-in-the-mouth pork cheeks worked fantastically well with the chocolate.

When I asked him whether he had watched Rick Stein's BBC series about Spain, he said he loved it, but complained that when Stein cooked on the programme it wasn't in the Spanish way. "It's a shame the UK still believes there's no space for a Spanish chef to go on TV and do a show and that they think they need to have someone like Rick Stein. Raymond Blanc goes to France, Gennaro Contaldo and Antonio Carluccio to Italy, Ken Hom to China, and Atul Kochhar to India. So why don't they have a Spanish chef go to Spain? Spanish food is the most popular in the UK right now. I just don't understand it."

In the clips I've watched of Omar cooking, he looks confident and, with his smiles and chatty tone, seems to be enjoying the experience. He's also made a short film for BBC1 about Benalmádena on the Costa del Sol ("It's literally the UK; it doesn't feel like Spain") with the food critic Jay Rayner. So why hasn't some TV company given him his own show?

"I've done a lot of showreels and trials with production companies but it hasn't happened", he said with a shrug, making no attempt to hide his disappointment.

I'm surprised his phone hasn't been ringing more often with calls from TV producers. He has everything needed to make the transition from restaurant kitchen to TV studio. He's charismatic, communicates his passion for Spanish food well, isn't fazed by the artificiality of cooking in front of cameras, and, with his beard and long hair, he looks the part.

It's clear that Omar would love to become a regular face on *Saturday Kitchen*, like José Pizarro, whom he admires but, at the same time, seems to consider a bit of a heretic. "José Pizarro doesn't give traditional recipes. He just uses fresh ingredients in his own way. It's a style of Spanish cuisine but it's not dishes with names. In Spain there is a big recipe book. José Pizarro might cook pan-fried cod with pesto and something else. It is Spanish food but it's not a Spanish dish. *Arroz meloso con verduras* is the title of a Spanish dish. *Lubina a la espalda* is the title of a Spanish dish. *Torrijas* is the title of a Spanish dish. What I cook are dishes that have a title, are recognisable, and that you will eat if you go to Spain. It would be great if José Pizarro did more dishes with a title."

Omar's talk about the importance of tradition reminded me of what

Paul Richardson wrote in his book, *A Late Dinner: Discovering the Food of Spain*: "The glittering edifice of the new Spanish food is built on the solid foundations of the old."

Omar might feel that he has been overlooked by producers, but I think it's just a matter of time before he becomes one of the faces of Spanish food on British TV and wins many converts. Since I met him, he has opened tapas bars in Sheffield and Birmingham and I'm sure he has plans to expand even more. "I want to bring real Spanish food to the people of England, not just to London. This is what I want to do in life."

3. The Adventurer

"Even ten years ago you wouldn't have put the words gastronomy and Spain in the same sentence."

Richard Bigg, Camino

If you go upstairs to the loo at Camino, behind Tate Modern on Bankside, you see three framed photos of a black Mini parked on a dusty road against a backdrop of olive trees. For Richard Bigg, the company's managing director, the photos aren't really about the car, although he loves cars: so much so that he was once a racing driver. The photos hang there to capture what was the beginning of a different love affair – with Spain.

"It was a really fun trip, but it wasn't successful from the girlfriend point of view, because we split up during it", he said, when I met him at the restaurant one lunchtime. "I drove across the country and it was, like, wow! The contrast, the heat, the diversity of landscapes and everything. I was in the completely wrong colour car, though, as it soaked up the heat. So I started going back, first once a year, then twice a year, three times a year, and eventually I bought a house in Andalusia."

With his shock of brown hair, white shirt, turquoise trousers, and brown leather satchel, Richard looked very youthful for someone who must be around the fifty mark. He also reminded me of one of those very English characters you would get in black and white movies about the Second World War. He might be under heavy attack from German artillery, or his ship might be slowly sinking, but he would always be cheerful and optimistic. "Come on, chaps! We're not beaten yet."

We were perched on black metal stools at a table outside. It felt a little precarious, as the table wobbled, something that happens in many restaurants with outside seating. Richard furrowed his brow and stood up to try and adjust it, but soon gave up. "I read that a three-legged table is the only answer. That never does this. But if that's the case, why doesn't everyone have them?"

A smiling young waitress wandered up to us armed with a small blackboard on which the specials were written. In a Spanish accent, she read out each one of them, along with the price. I wondered if she knew that she was serving the boss. Richard asked me what I'd like to eat and I said I was happy to go with his choices. If the owner of a restaurant doesn't know what's good to eat, then who does? He ordered *chipirones* (baby squid) with *alioli* and lemon, Cornish hake with mushroom and peas, goat's cheese with quince jelly, *gazpacho*, and Ibérico ham.

What appealed to him on that trip was the contrast between England and Spain. "I'm English and I adore it. But I found Spain intoxicating. I loved the way some regions were full of forest and mountains and others were dead flat. I literally drove from the north to the south, and I was just amazed. I love England for what it is, which is a very equable climate: it's soft, it's green, it's a little bit hilly. But these were stark mountain ranges. Spain is the second most mountainous country in Europe after Switzerland. As a result, some of it is super hot and some of it super cold. This temperature range is great for the vines, because it's hot in the day time and then it cools down at night."

During the trip, he stayed with a school friend at the friend's mum's house in Madrid and experienced what seems to be have been a life changing moment. "One night she said, 'You're not allowed back because my boyfriend's coming around. Don't come back until nine in the morning.' We thought, OK, that's fine. By about six in the morning we were feeling really weary, but then you do what any Spaniard would do after a big night out. You have some *churros* with chocolate. It was a sensational thing to eat, and really gave me energy."

The *churros* told him that if a country can produce something so simple and delicious, then it was worth taking a look at what else it had to offer. "Slowly, over the years, I realised that there were a lot of contrasts in Spanish food. It's so diverse. There are dishes in the south you would never get in the north and vice versa. Each area has its own strong identity in terms of food that matches it – I love the way that happens, not just in Spain but also in Italy and France."

When he said this, I remembered HV Morton in *A Stranger in Spain* quoting an old Spanish saying: "In the south they fry, in the centre they roast, and in the north they stew." Others talk about the food of the sea, the food of the plains, and the food of the mountains.

Richard's passion for Spain, ignited on that trip thirty years ago, coupled with what you might call a boyish enthusiasm, is the driving force of Camino, one of a wave of trendy and stylish Spanish restaurants that have sprung up across central London in the last few years. Its first branch opened in Kings Cross in 2007 and was followed by two branches in the City, at Mincing Lane and Blackfriars Lane. In addition, it runs a sherry bar, Bar Pepito, next to its Kings Cross restaurant and, beside the Blackfriars branch, Copa de Cava, which Richard claims is London's first cava bar. He closed a Canary Wharf branch in 2014 after plans to build two tall towers nearby failed to materialise.

The popularity of Spanish food in London has attracted the money men. Camino's expansion has been helped by a three million pound investment from the Business Growth Fund, owned by some of Britain's biggest banks. This is serious money, but then food is a serious business. We all need to eat. And if you can come up with the right formula, then there's big money to be made.

Camino restaurants are designed to be fun places, reflecting Richard's love of the bar environment. The Bankside restaurant, which was previously a Mediterranean deli and brasserie, had been open only three weeks. Inside, it was bright and spacious, with the bar flanked by an open kitchen on one side and on the other by a *jamón* counter, containing an intriguing old machine with a rotating blade to slice the ham.

He chose the name Camino, roughly translated as "path", because it's a link between all the places in Spain he's visited. "I was on the *camino*, travelling, and did dozens and dozens of road trips. I must have been to Spain about a hundred times. I'm told by Spaniards I work with that I know Spain better than them. I've made the effort to explore it. In fact, I know Spain far better than I know England. I'm hazy on my geography of England. Like any subject the more you learn the more you realise you don't know. But I know quite a bit about Spain and I want to take more road trips to explore it."

He suggested that you never see a bar in Spain described as a tapas bar. Bars are simply bars that serve tapas. Richard maintained that it originated in Seville. "Seville is pretty much at sea level and on the Guadalquivir River it is super hot and very humid, so there are a lot of flies. You don't want the flies going in your drink so you put a lid over it. It was just a bit of bread. Then after a while people thought, let's put a bit of ham on it. And then they decided to put a bit of cheese, anchovy, or tomato on it. Eventually they put all this on plates. This is how it originally began. It was bar food, small bites. Also, because it was so hot, you didn't want to eat heavy meals." He broke off and made a puzzled expression. "What I don't understand is that while the flies don't get into your drink, they can get to your food.

"Tapas ticks a lot of boxes because it's casual dining", he continued, taking a sip from a glass of Mahou beer, which he believes should always be served in half pint glasses so it stays nice and crisp and cold. "Tapas is small plates, it's sharing, it's informal, and you can eat as many dishes as you want or as few as you want. This is exactly what we want to encourage here. You can drop by at any time of the day, have a little glass of beer or a glass of wine, a slice of *tortilla*, a quick lunch, or a business lunch. And you can drop by in the evening after work and end up staying all night. Your mates can rock up. It's just a bar. And I love this informality."

No one can touch Spain when it comes to food and wine, he argued. "Even ten years ago you wouldn't have put the words gastronomy and Spain in the same sentence. In Spain they are incredibly innovative. They have fantastic produce and you don't have to mess around with it too much to create wonderful dishes. For the last seven or eight years, in *Restaurant* magazine's Top Fifty, there have been more Spanish places in the top ten than from any other country. This year there were two in the top ten and there wasn't any other country with more than one. This is high-end cuisine, and it isn't what everyone wants to eat or what every restaurateur wants to do. But this sends a very powerful message about Spanish food, and that filters down."

Richard was right when he said British people have always had a good feeling when they think of Spain, because they associate it with sea, beaches, and sun. But now they are also associating it with good food. When the waitress brought two bowls of bright orange *gazpacho*, Richard whipped his phone out of his jacket pocket. "I'll take some snaps for the chef. He'd like to get the feedback." I'd read about how delicious *gazpacho* was supposed to be, but had never tried it before. It was an absolute revelation. It was so silky and refreshing,

Keeping things simple seems to be one of Richard's guiding principles, which is why he decided to have a short wine list and to make it easy to understand. "Choose the very best and have a wide range of styles in the shortest possible number. I think this is a much more friendly and helpful way of doing things than trying to bewilder people."

He extolled the virtues of sherry and suggested most wine experts would choose to take a good sherry, over wine, if they were to be stranded on a desert island. "In my opinion, sherry is the best food-matching wine there is, and it's very diverse. We do flights of sherry and little tasting menus, six different food items matched with six different sherries, with fifty millilitre glasses. It's a little crash course in sherry."

Despite his love for and fascination with Spain, Richard had what sounds like a very English upbringing in Hampshire, Kent, and Sussex. His father worked for a brewery before setting up his own business. "At one point, we had a little keg of beer in the house, which was better than having it in bottles. If you nicked a bottle, he would probably notice. But he wouldn't if you took a cheeky glass from the keg. He wouldn't let us drink beer, but he seemed to think cider was all right. I remember we had crates of cider in the house."

Given that food in most homes in England back then wasn't particularly inspiring or imaginative, his mother was adventurous in the kitchen, cooking dishes such as lasagne and moussaka. Richard rubbed his chin and wondered aloud whether his parents had a subliminal influence on his career: his mother the food and his father the drink.

At the age of eleven he went to a Steiner school. The Austrian Rudolf Steiner, who founded the system, believed that each day should begin with the "morning birth", something designed to help pupils think positively about the day ahead and work together. Richard described himself as "a very average student". After leaving school, he left home and, through his father's connections, got a job in a factory in Munich for six months. When he returned to England, he put on a suit and worked for a commodities company in the City, but became disillusioned by the daily grind and the low pay. This was when he took off in his black Mini to explore Spain.

Still restless, he then flew to South America, backpacking around Peru, Bolivia, Chile, and Argentina before heading up to the United States. He bought a motorbike and took to the road, travelling through twenty-eight states and doing various jobs. He did a stint as a bartender in Long Island where, because of the tips, he made more money than he had as a commodities trader. I was a little surprised when he went on to tell me that he had worked as a labourer at a ski resort in Colorado.

"It was out of season and full of some real live cowboys", he explained. "I was in a bar when one of them challenged me to an arm wrestle for a round of drinks. I declined, thinking I had no chance whatsoever, and said he could just have the drinks. He insisted, however, so off we set, and somehow I managed to beat him. It was clear he hadn't expected this outcome, but he was true to his word and said in a slow drawl, 'Boy, you beat me fair and square,' and paid for the round."

"Sounds like you had a few adventures", I said.

"I did. I got beaten up in New Orleans by the police", he mentioned casually.

"How?" I asked. Richard doesn't seem the sort of guy to get on the wrong side of the police.

"Oh, they were doing a stakeout. Anyway, it was just one of those things", he said with a flick of the hand. "Then when I got to Texas my motorbike fell apart. It was car and Greyhound buses after that."

After returning to London, he found a job at the Dome Café Bar in Islington, where he was taught a valuable lesson. "It was owned by Trusthouse Forte and the great message I learned was how not to treat your staff. They were poor about paying people well and showing appreciation. Thankfully this kind of management is firmly out of the window now. You can't possibly survive if you don't respect your staff."

He was a lousy waiter, he confessed, and he couldn't understand how chefs did what they did in the kitchen. "I have a tremendous respect for chefs. I don't know how they keep so calm under pressure and don't shout at the staff. Maintaining quality and consistency is a huge challenge for a chef."

Eventually he quit the Dome, working for "another couple of dodgy restaurants" and trying his hand as a motorbike dispatch rider and water filter salesman. By now he was in his mid-twenties and felt he wasn't going anywhere in life or making much money.

When he got a job at a sports car showroom in Lancaster Gate, someone suggested he took up racing. So, using some inheritance from his grandmother, he became a Formula Ford driver, considered by some, he says, to be a step between go-karting and Formula One. "The cars were fast because they were low to the ground and single-seater. The handling was incredible because they were super lightweight." However, after a year, he ran out of money and was forced to abandon this exciting career.

By now an idea had formed in his mind and he could see a new path opening up before him. "The only thing I wanted to do was open my own bar and do things my way." Despite his wife's lack of enthusiasm for the venture, Richard went ahead and remortgaged his house and, as a result, the marriage collapsed. He teamed up with Nigel Foster, a business partner he met through a mutual friend. "We complement each other really well. He's an entrepreneur who is involved in several businesses and very successful. When I told him that numbers and accounts terrified me, he said that's OK, you just hire an accountant.

He's a lovely chap, so we're friends as well as business partners. But it's important that we were business partners first. There's that old saying that you should never do business with friends. And it's such a truism. Never ever do it. There's one friendship I completely lost when I went into a business with a friend. It was a terrible shame, as he was the best man at my second wedding."

In 1995, going on gut instinct, he opened a bar called Cantaloupe in Shoreditch. Rent was low as, back then, Shoreditch hadn't become the kind of trendy area it is today. The bar was an immediate success, scooping *Time Out*'s Bar of the Year award. A second venue, Cargo, soon followed, located under nearby railway arches. It offered live music and – a first for London, claims Richard – street food.

Having discovered his niche, Richard then got involved in The Big Chill music festival, in the grounds of Eastnor Castle in Herefordshire. He ran the bar side of the event, which attracted 40,000 people in three and a half days. "We had eleven bars and 350 bartenders. The logistics were horrific. It was an experience, but I wouldn't do it again."

By this point, he was running Cantaloupe, Cargo, another venue called Market Place, two Big Chill bars, and the festival. On the face of it, he had finally arrived, but he found it all a bit too much. "I would change the menu in one place, change the staff, and I thought, this is too complicated. It was so stressful and so much work. I thought, what has happened to my dream? My dream was to open my own bar. And now we're doing nightclubs, DJ bars, festivals. People say, 'God, that was a legend. It was the first place in Shoreditch. It was wild with people dancing on tables.' We had Czech beer, Mediterranean food. But actually, it wouldn't work today. Its identity then was that it was in the wild East End, which it wasn't, because Shoreditch isn't the East End."

That memorable journey through Spain all those years before kept coming back to him. So he suggested to Nigel Foster that they open a tapas bar. "There weren't many tapas bars in London and most were pretty dreadful. They had been opened by Spanish people who had come over decades before and the menu would be pretty boring. It was meatballs, poor *patatas bravas* or *paella*, and so on. It wasn't very adventurous. I had a good feeling about opening a tapas bar. I recognised that Spain was the number one holiday destination for British people and many went to live there, so it would be an easy sell. It wasn't like selling Romanian country food or something. I loved the tapas style of eating. But above all I just had a burning passion to do it and was following my instincts again."

While he was talking, we were eating, and the food was fantastic. The problem with sharing tapas, though, is knowing how much to eat. When you are eating food as good as this, you want more, but you don't want to risk appearing greedy. So I was careful not to eat too much, something I think Richard sensed. "Just tidy that one up", he said, pointing to the baby squid as a waitress arrived with the hake.

Camino doesn't have a target market, he insisted. "When we had our branding meeting we discussed who was our target customer, and what is the demographic. And we realised there isn't one. You can't pigeonhole people. People might regard it as a meal and come for an evening to one of our restaurants and spend a lot of money, or they might pop in for a quick snack and spend a tenner. We like the idea that people can use tapas any way they want, to cater for all ages. I come with my family at the weekend and there are kids charging around. And I bring my mum here."

He sees each of Camino's locations as very different because of the people who live and work there. "We have a place in the City where people from the insurance companies come and spend well and have really good lunches. Here on Bankside there are a lot of people who work in publishing. Kings Cross is a real night time destination and the people who come have a lot of energy. We have dancing and a DJ. On Thursday and Friday nights there we turn the tables two and a half times."

As we were chatting, voices inside the restaurant began singing "Happy Birthday".

"Can you hear that?" he said, cocking his head and breaking into a smile. "That's great, isn't it!"

Like most people, I'd always thought that Billingsgate market was the place to go to buy fresh fish. But Richard doesn't buy from Billingsgate because, he believes, much of it is frozen and comes from other countries, not from the British coast. All his fresh fish comes from a small family fishing business in Cornwall and is delivered directly to the restaurant. The octopus comes from the north Atlantic. At one time, he refused to put anchovies on the menu because they were dredged, but he eventually found some that were sustainable. Nevertheless, he buys frozen prawns from the Far East, because it would be too expensive to buy fresh ones.

When it comes to buying vegetables, he tries to ensure as far as possible that they are home grown. "I would never have Peruvian asparagus, for example, as asparagus is such a classic dish. I always think, with vegetables: English where possible, but not beyond Europe. I just think that's wrong. All the global warming and pollution that come from buying vegetables from the other side of the planet are insane." His executive chef, Nacho del Campo, shares this philosophy. He isn't concerned, like some chefs, with making sure that vegetables are all cut the same size or have the perfect shape.

Given the high costs of setting up a restaurant in central London, how long is it before Richard expects Camino Bankside to make a profit? He said confidently that it shouldn't take longer than four years.

Continuing to expand Camino is part of his vision. "The reason for this is that it energises the company, and the people who work in it get very excited and their careers develop. It also provides new opportunities for people coming into the company. Someone might join as a bartender or pot-washer and then become a manager and earn more money. If you can demonstrate that you are a company that is doing well and expanding, then people want to be a part of that. It just makes you feel better about the company you work for. There's absolutely nothing wrong with opening one really good bar and restaurant and just doing that, but you will have to change staff from time to time, as people will want to move on."

He hadn't forgotten the year he spent working at the Dome in Islington. "Whatever we do with the design, the food, and the drink, the number one thing is the staff. No matter how much you like the food when you go to a restaurant, if it's served by surly staff that just plonk the dishes down in front of you and walk off, you won't go back. Why should you? But staff aren't going to serve you well unless they have had the right sort of training. And you need to employ the right kind of person. You don't want to put a square peg in a round hole. You need to be a people person, someone who is sociable, smiling, engaging, confident, and relaxed."

I asked what the difference is between a group of restaurants and a chain. "It's the same concept, but a chain sounds very cold, and as if it's run by people who don't care and don't have a passion for the business. A group is where the staff are more important than the customers."

Since opening the first branch of Camino, he has taken staff on twice-yearly trips to Spain. He added, with some pride, that he has missed only two. "Around a dozen go each time and they visit a winery or *bodega*, and also a city. The idea is to immerse the staff in

Spanish food, drink, and culture. It's an absolute revelation. And I get a real kick out of taking Spaniards to a part of Spain they don't know. Often it's the first time some of the staff have been to a winery or seen how wine is made."

I liked the idea of taking staff on trips to see where the produce they serve comes from, and you can see why it makes sense. If the staff can talk about the menu with knowledge and understanding, it helps create a good experience for the customer. For the staff, the trips increase their confidence in what they are selling and make them feel that the company is investing in them. Richard said that when his staff come back after a trip, "they are absolutely glowing."

He travels to Spain five or six times a year, because of the staff trips and because his girlfriend comes from Barbastro in Aragón. "I met her by chance when I was travelling through Spain in a van, collecting things to decorate Camino and chucking them in the back. She was working in a restaurant and the antique shop next door. Someone had recommended that I drop by."

Social media has, of course, become an important tool in marketing restaurants. With so much competition in London you have to get out there and entice customers, offering special deals and even putting on events. "It used to be that to have a successful restaurant you just need amazing food, brilliant staff, a fantastic looking venue, and brilliant drinks. But now you need all those things and amazing social media as well. Any of the new exciting businesses that are opening up tend to be fantastic in using social media. It's hard to put a percentage on it, but I reckon those four original factors add up to no more than two thirds of what's going to make you appeal to the public. They need to hear about you. You need to be on Facebook and Twitter and all the social media platforms."

According to Richard, the whole eating out scene is better in London than in any other city in the world, and this is spreading to other parts of the country. "It's more diverse. There's so much innovation: so much energy, passion. For a country not known for its gastronomic prowess, Britain is absolutely on fire."

He's a member of the "Tortilla Club", a small group of people involved in Spanish food in London who go on occasional tapas trails. "There are a lot of very good Spanish places in London and most of us know each other and are friendly with each other and respect each other. We all try very hard to be as good as we can."

As we ended the meal with an espresso accompanied by a shot of brandy, Richard said that, at one time in Britain, food was just fuel and was never adventurous. "But, boy, look at us now! Look at the diversity and the quality of restaurants in London. It's something else. The English are right up there."

As I packed away my tape recorder and notebook, he invited me to come inside the restaurant and see the photos of the Mini. As we went up the stairs, he paused and, studying the photos, said reflectively, "Half a dozen of us from head office sat down with Gus González, our marketing and social media manager, and we were talking about the importance of the brand. During the conversation he said to me, 'Richard, you've opened a Spanish place, despite the fact that you're English. So the fact that you've chosen Spain is very powerful. You could have chosen any other country.' This was a very good point."

4. Miss Tapas

"I thought it would be nice to open a tapas bar here, the same kind of place I would go to in Seville."

Blanca Rowe, Miss Tapas

It would be hard to think of two places more different from each other than Seville and Peckham: one in the south of Spain, the other in the south of London. Seville conjures up images of narrow streets, fountains, and churches, with the smell of orange blossom in the air and the sound of flamenco drifting from a small bar by the river; Peckham conjures up images of cheap shops, scruffy buildings, and teenage gangs posing on YouTube. Seville is immortalised in the operas, Carmen and The Barber of Seville; Peckham was the setting for the TV comedies, *Only Fools and Horses* and *Desmond's*. Seville has a magnificent cathedral and the sweeping Plaza de España, with its arches, towers, and small bridges; Peckham has a branch of Primark and a bus garage.

I remember going to the North Peckham Estate when I worked as a researcher on a Channel 4 TV programme some years ago, and it was one of the worst examples of Sixties architecture you could imagine. With its low-rise concrete blocks linked by long walkways, it looked more like a fortress than somewhere people lived. Because of drugs, muggings, burglaries, and violence, the estate was regarded as one of the most dangerous in London. Postmen and milkmen were scared to go there. Some flats were boarded up and many of the windows on the ground floors had been fitted with bars. It was one of the most desolate, depressing places you could imagine.

We had gone to film a small Catholic community of brothers who were living in a flat and hoping, with the kind of optimism particular to people with deep religious faith, to be a positive presence in the area. As we parked our Transit van and made our way up a flight of urine-smelling steps to the community's flat, we figured that, by filming in daylight, we would be OK. We were wrong. While we were in the flat with the brothers, discussing what to film, someone broke into the van and fled with a camera and other expensive equipment. When the police arrived, they noted down the details of the stolen gear, but shrugged and said there was little chance of recovering any of it. This kind of thing happened in Peckham all the time, it seemed.

Given all this, Peckham might seem an odd choice of location to open the kind of small tapas bar that you find in Seville. Yet that's exactly what Blanca Rowe has done. Situated down a shabby side street, Miss Tapas looks distinctly out of place among the shops and cafés with names like The Merciful God African Food (Wholesale and Retail), Humble Worldwide Shipping African Ltd (Door to Door), Oritis Cosmetics, and Lolak Afrique Restaurant.

These businesses reflect Peckham's status as the home of Britain's largest Nigerian community. Wander along Rye Lane, its narrow, crowded main street, and you'll see halal butchers selling goat's feet, smoked chicken, and tripe; stalls piled high with sweet potatoes, okra, yams, and plantains; and shops selling wigs, colourful traditional Nigerian clothes, and West African DVDs. While Peckham doesn't have a medieval cathedral like Seville, it boasts numerous African churches, located in industrial estates, nightclubs, and former shops, with names like The Celestial Church of Miracles and Winners, and Praise the Redeemer on Mount Zion.

Blanca's decision to open a tapas bar in Peckham isn't as far-fetched as it might appear. Peckham, like so many previously unfashionable parts of London, has been changing in recent years. The North Peckham Estate has been demolished and replaced by new houses. In Bellenden Road, artists' studios and vintage clothing shops have opened up, and estate agents call it "Bellenden Village" to try to distance it from the less attractive parts of Peckham. There are hipster cafés in Peckham Rye, and one on the tenth floor of a multi-storey car park. Families unable to afford the more desirable properties in neighbouring East Dulwich, with its restaurants and wine shops, have been snapping up flats and Victorian houses in Peckham, sending property prices soaring and introducing something never seen here before: bicycles with baskets on the front. It's these sort of people who would choose to go to a tapas bar.

I arrived at the bar one morning to find Blanca, a petite young woman dressed in Lycra leggings, busy unpacking a box. "I don't usually dress like this when I'm here", she apologised, explaining that she had been to the gym.

Bars and restaurants create their own vibe, and as soon as I walked through the door of Miss Tapas I immediately liked it. It's small, with just a few tables, and each of them has stools, so it's definitely a bar and not a restaurant. It's the kind of place where you could easily strike up a conversation with the people sitting at the next table, which is the general idea. On the walls are black and white photos of street scenes in Seville and framed posters from two of its famous annual festivals, Semana Santa and the Feria de Abril.

"You know, when I came to London, I realised that if I wanted Spanish food I would have to wait until I went back to Spain", Blanca said as we sat down. "It was too expensive and you didn't get the real taste."

There are no printed menus at Miss Tapas. Instead, what's on offer each day is written on chalk boards. Among the items that day were quail egg with *chorizo* and Spanish fried chicken.

"We're not serving funky or crazy dishes. It's just what I ate in Spain", she explained. Her most popular dishes are *patatas bravas*, *tortilla*, and *presa ibérica de bellota*, served medium rare, which people assume is beef, not pork. She also offers salads, because she doesn't want people to think Spanish food is just meat. "We are a big meat country, especially in the south, but we also eat a lot of fish and vegetables."

Everything at Miss Tapas, from the kitchen to the menu, is small: the wine list offers seven red, five white, one rosé, and one sparkling, as well as six sherries. Unsurprisingly, Rioja is the best seller, although Goru from Jumilla in Murcia is also popular, she said. "We sell more red than white – I was told when I went to my wine supplier that English people drink more white than red. Many people think sherry is for old people, but when they try it they love it."

Blanca grew up in Seville, the capital of Andalusia and the largest city in southern Spain. Despite its history and beautiful buildings, I suspect that, for many people, the big attraction of Seville is its tapas bars. I've heard that it has around 3,000. This might be an exaggeration, but its streets are packed with them. If you wander through the city in the evening, you'll see crowded bars and people standing at outdoor tables, everyone having a wonderful time and, unlike in England, no one behaving stupidly. While we like to think of Seville as a city of fun and romance, outside its historic centre it has more in common with Peckham than might at first be apparent. I can remember the time I travelled by road to Seville from Extremadura and was taken aback, when we reached the northern edge of the city, by the run-down housing developments, with graffiti scrawled on the walls and rubbish strewn around. When I read *Ghosts of Spain* by Giles Tremlett, I discovered that Seville has many such estates, housing around 60,000 people.

But this is not the Seville Blanca wants to bring to Peckham. Going out in Seville in the evening for tapas might, for her, mean meeting a group of friends then starting with a drink and slice of *tortilla* at the popular Bodeguita del Salvador – one of several bars in the Plaza del Salvador – before moving on to Blanco Cerillo, from where the smell of hake, whitebait, and other fish, marinated in vinegar, *pimentón*, cumin, and bay leaf, and served in a paper cone, would waft enticingly down the street. After that, it would be a case of wherever the mood took her.

She talked nostalgically about two dishes that take her right back to the flavours of her childhood in Seville: *salmorejo* and *puchero*. *Salmorejo* is a cold soup, similar to but thicker than *gazpacho*, and is made with tomatoes, bread, garlic, olive oil, and vinegar. This is typically eaten in the summer, when the temperature in Seville soars. *Puchero*, on the other hand, is a winter dish. It's a stew made with pork, chicken, beef, fish bones, chick peas, and vegetables. It's eaten with bread or very thin pasta. In the days when Spain was poor, people would make a big pot of this and it would last for several days.

As much as she loves her native Seville, Blanca was eager for adventure and new experiences. After spells working at a travel agent and for a PR company, she came to London five years ago. "If I had stayed in Seville, I would have known exactly how my life would develop. I thought, I'm twenty-six and I don't want such a predictable life: getting a job, finding a boyfriend, getting married, and buying a house." She worked for a family as an au pair, attending a language school in Oxford Street to learn English. However, after a year she realised her English wasn't improving that much, because she spent most of her time with a small child and, when she went out, she met up with Spanish friends.

Anxious to do something more stimulating, she landed a job at Itsu, a Japanese restaurant chain, in the City. And she met her fiancé. When he invited her to go to a Spanish restaurant on their first date, she admits that she wasn't that enthusiastic, thinking that Spanish food in London wouldn't be anything as good as what she ate back home. "He took me to José in Bermondsey Street. And I really loved it. Then I got an idea in my mind: I thought it would be good to have more places like this. It wasn't as cheap as Spain, but the prices weren't crazy." Soon afterwards, she decided to set up a Jamón Ibérico business with a teacher friend, importing it from Jabugo, a town in Andalusia famous for its ham. She went out visiting restaurants, leaving samples and hoping for orders, but soon learned that it was hard to make a living from this.

It was when she and her boyfriend moved to Peckham in 2014 that she saw another opportunity: opening a tapas bar. Her fiancé knew a few things about restaurants, as he and a friend had set up a successful chain of burrito outlets, cashing in on that other recent feature of the London culinary scene: the craze for Mexican food.

"I realised the area was really nice and the community was lovely", she said. "I thought it would be nice to open a tapas bar here, the same kind of place I would go to in Seville. So we started looking for a premises. I posted letters through doors, saying I was looking for a property to turn into a bar." Her imaginative approach paid off. One day she received a phone call from someone with a place to rent. He said that when he had arrived back from New York he had two letters waiting for him, one from the owner of the cake shop he rented out saying that he was leaving and one from Blanca.

So did she do any research to see whether a tapas bar might be viable in Peckham? "I knew what I wanted. I wanted a tapas bar in London. I didn't do a study of the market. In my head it was so clear. I wanted to create the kind of tapas bar I knew in Seville and I wanted to be part of a community. If you want to make money, then you open a restaurant in Soho or Shoreditch. But you won't get that neighbourhood feeling there, because there are new people all the time. I have regulars and it's nice to chat with them about their kids or their holidays. And I like that, because that's what happens in Seville."

Blanca and her fiancé managed to scrape together enough money to take on the lease. As they couldn't afford to hire professionals, they had to do much of the refurbishment work themselves. A friend who was an engineer helped them with the lighting and plumbing and Blanca bought the wood from a Peckham timber merchant, the stools and lights from eBay, and the tiles from a shop in East Dulwich.

Pointing to the wall, she said proudly, "I put those bricks there", and took out her mobile phone to show me photos of her and her fiancé gutting the shop.

When I suggested that opening a restaurant must be quite risky, especially for someone with no experience, she replied that because it's small she didn't feel overwhelmed at the prospect. All the same, she had a few sleepless nights. "When you do something for the first time it's always really hard. At the beginning, I was really stressed because I wanted to be like someone who had been running a restaurant for a few years. I thought to myself I have to do this and I have to do that. And you get frustrated and worried. I could have organised my time better."

Working at Itsu provided her with valuable knowledge about how to run a restaurant effectively, not least in ensuring that it is cleaned properly and that health and safety regulations are adhered to.

So how did she find a chef? "When I was planning to open I asked a friend of mine who ran restaurants in Seville and he recommended Manuel, who was working in Ibiza at the time. We now have another chef, from Valencia, who joined us last week."

At the beginning, she operated a booking system, but ended up with a half empty restaurant, so she got rid of it. "If you do everything with care and love and you make mistakes, it's not that bad. You can learn from your mistakes. If you don't make mistakes, you don't learn."

Her former flatmate, Anna, who comes from Sanlúcar de Barrameda on Andalusia's Atlantic coast, takes care of the bar when Blanca isn't there. "Even though it's my restaurant I see myself as part of the team. You have to listen to the people who work for you. You have to make them happy or you can't make the people who come through the doors happy. If your staff are happy, then everyone will be happy."

Like most of us, Blanca hates it when she goes to a restaurant and a waiter begins pressuring her to leave because he wants the table for other customers. That's why she's happy for people to linger as long as they want in her bar, like they do in Seville. "I don't like to tell people that they have to leave. It's not Spanish. When you are enjoying yourself you can spend the whole evening in the bar. I don't mind – so long as you are not drinking water."

Tapas is about bringing people together but it can also, unintentionally, keep them apart. You won't find many Nigerians sitting on the stools at Miss Tapas and tucking into a dish of *boquerones* (cured anchovies). Blanca wonders whether this might be because they don't eat pork. I think it's something more universal. When I visited Spain for the first time, I searched for restaurants with pizza or pasta on the menu. I didn't know much about Spanish food, so I looked for what was familiar. It's natural that, when people are away from home, they want to maintain a connection with it, and there's no better way than through food. In some ways, this is what Blanca has done by bringing a Seville tapas bar to Peckham. Yet I can't help feeling that the Nigerians in Peckham don't know what they are missing.

"Everyone leaves the restaurant happy, and that is my aim", Blanca confided. "I don't want to disappoint people. It's like when you are preparing a dinner in your house and you burn something. Of course, you can't please everyone. When you have a good time in a restaurant it's down to the food, the service, and the atmosphere. With every single person I serve, I imagine I am serving myself. So I wouldn't serve anything I wouldn't eat."

Of course, running a restaurant is about making money, she acknowledged, but it doesn't have to be just about that. "I know I'm not going to get rich at this. I'm going to make enough money to pay rent, pay salaries, and make a bit of profit", said Blanca.

She lives a few streets away, which means she isn't faced with a long commute each day, unlike many Londoners. Given that she is usually at the bar from the morning until mid-afternoon and then back in the evening, this is important. After her ham supplier from Seville visited the bar, he texted to congratulate her on creating an authentic Seville bar. This meant a lot to her.

Blanca is a good example of a young entrepreneur with a passion for good Spanish food, who wants to share it with others. It's still early days for her tapas bar and she will have to navigate the usual problems associated with establishing a restaurant and building up a loyal group of customers. But at least she's found a reliable fishmonger now. I hope she succeeds, because Peckham needs its little bit of Seville.

5. It's Not Just Rioja

"Actually the wine that is selling best for us is a Syrah, or a Shiraz, from Arribes del Duero, near Salamanca. This is showing an international varietal in a region most people haven't heard of."

Dave Green, The Haciendas Company

I will always remember the first time I drank a Spanish wine, because – I'm ashamed to say – I can't remember what I did afterwards. I was meeting a friend at a bar on Tower Bridge Road, on one of those hot summer afternoons when London is teeming with Japanese and American tourists with cameras hanging around their necks. As he spent much of his time flying around the world giving motivational talks in churches, schools, and prisons, I rarely got to see him, so I was looking forward to having a few beers and catching up.

When I arrived, he was sitting at a table in the corner. "Listen! You've got to try this", he said, pointing to the bottle of red wine in front of him.

"What is it?" I said, peering at the label, as I squeezed into my seat.

"A Rioja. It's fantastic!"

I'd heard the name Rioja, of course, but felt foolish for not knowing much about it. Did it refer to a grape, a type of wine, a region, or a brand? Swept along by my friend's enthusiasm, I abandoned my planned trip to the bar for a pint of lager and allowed him to pour me a glass.

"What do you reckon?"

When I took a sip, the taste was astonishing. It wasn't harsh and bitter, like most of the wines I'd tried previously. It was like tasting a rich cream dessert, and it felt as smooth as silk. "Wow!" I said.

"Told you, didn't I? I'd never tried Rioja until someone took me to a restaurant in Paris last year. I love it now."

As the afternoon drifted by, our glasses kept emptying and, by the time we walked unsteadily out of the bar, we had polished off no fewer than five bottles. We paid the bill, said our goodbyes, and I just about remember standing on the pavement, blinking in the sunshine, as my friend wobbled off over Tower Bridge to his hotel.

When I woke up the next morning, I couldn't remember much of what we'd talked about, but I remembered the taste of the Rioja, and my tongue was a deep purple colour. Later that day, I popped into my local Tesco, where I found four different Riojas on the shelves. I studied the labels of each one, but didn't have a clue what the differences were, so, of course, I just bought the cheapest.

The whole business of wine labels can be very confusing. You know where you are if you are buying cans of beer or lager. It's just that: beer or lager produced by different breweries. But with wine you have to decode the information on the label. You might have the name of the producer, the brand, the name of the winery, the region, the variety of grape, the year the grapes were harvested, the style, and maybe the name of the estate where the wine was bottled. And the information available varies from country to country. Bottles from France, for example, don't always list the grape. Faced with all of this, it's no wonder that many of us are wary about buying an unfamiliar wine.

It's not just wine labels that can leave you scratching your head. It's also the systems countries operate for classifying wine. In Europe, the production of wine is tightly controlled to ensure that claims about the geographical area it comes from are accurate, and to guarantee its quality. Spain introduced the Denominación de Origen (DO) system in 1932, which is similar to the Appellation d'Origine Contrôlée in France and Italy's Denominazione di Origine Controllata. Spain now has sixty-nine DOs and, more recently, a higher category, Denominaciones de Origen Calificada (labelled DOCa), was introduced, so far awarded only to Rioja and Priorat. To make matters more complicated, the Spanish system has four other categories: Vino de Mesa, Vino de la Tierra, Vinos de Calidad con Indicación Geográfica, and Vino de Pago.

Despite our confusion about wine, we love drinking it, perhaps reflecting the way aspirations have changed and how we see ourselves, and want to be seen. Britain is now the sixth biggest consumer of wine in the world. Arguably, this change in drinking habits can be traced back to the 1970s, when people began holding cheese and wine parties and forsaking "kiss me quick" British seaside resorts for holidays overseas, especially to Spain.

Even though my parents never drank wine when I was growing up, this being something posh people did, I do have a strong memory of it. This was because my mum would drag me off to Mass each Sunday and, once I was seven, I would take a sip from the chalice the priest held at communion. I found its smell mysterious and strangely appealing. But, of course, you weren't meant to think of it as wine. It was supposed to be the blood of Jesus.

I started to get into wine only after watching Rick Stein's TV programmes about Spain. Up until then, I had been a confirmed lager drinker. The only time I had drunk wine had been at receptions, book launches, or other similar events you sometimes get invited to as a journalist. I don't recall ever drinking anything I liked. This might have been because at most of those events they bought the cheapest wine available.

At one time, wines from France, Italy, and the New World overshadowed those from Spain. Many considered Spanish wine little more than cheap plonk. In the 1971 edition of *The World Atlas of Wine*, Hugh Johnson described the Spanish wine industry as "desultory" and concluded that, with a few exceptions, such as Rioja and sherry, "Spanish wine is just wine".

He wouldn't say that today. Sarah Jane Evans, Master of Wine and one of the judges at the Decanter World Wine Awards 2015, declared that Spain is "the most exciting thing happening in European wine right now". According to 2015 statistics from the International Organisation of Vine and Wine, Spain is now the third largest producer of wine in the world, with only Italy and France producing more. Over half of Spain's wine production comes not from La Rioja, as many people think, but from Castilla-La Mancha. La Rioja is, in fact, only the fifth largest producing region, behind Catalonia, Extremadura, and Valencia.

Because Spain has such a diverse terrain and climate, it produces a wide variety of wine. At the north-west end there is what's known as green Spain, a cold and wet area, which stretches from the Atlantic to the Pyrenees. In Andalusia in the south there is the opposite. In this region, looking out towards Africa, the temperature soars in summer and the land becomes arid. In between these extremes there are the Ebro river valley and Duero river valley in the north, and the central plateau – known as the table top – on which Madrid proudly sits. Adding to this diversity are the Mediterranean coast on the east and the Canary and Balearic Islands.

I'd heard that Phil Amery at Albion Wines was someone who knew a thing or two about Spanish wine, so I arranged to see him. I met him in the cluttered office at the back of his shop in Lamb's Conduit Street, which, with its florist, funeral director, bike shop, and attractive pubs, has a village feel about it. Appropriately, it's near Gray's Inn, home to some of London's barristers and judges, who are well known for liking a tipple.

When you enter the shop you have to be careful not to trip over. There are bottles of wine everywhere. It might appear chaotic, but the idea is to encourage customers to root around. This, combined with the fading colourful poster of a Mexican vineyard (the shop used to sell Mexican wine) and a wall map of the wine regions of Spain, gives the shop an old-fashioned charm. You could almost imagine you were in a Dickens novel.

A jovial man in his late fifties, Phil comes across as someone always struggling with a long to-do list and perhaps wondering where he last left his pen. He told me that Spanish wine has grown enormously in popularity in the last few years and now accounts for around fifty per cent of Albion Wines' sales. "Spain is a terrific area to be buying wine at the moment, because its domestic market is absolutely shot to pieces", he claimed. "If you go to Bordeaux, Burgundy, or wherever, you can have one bottle of wine that is terrific and a second bottle which is diabolical. Spanish wine is more consistent."

Spain is offering really great value, he said. "You can get wines twenty to twenty-five per cent cheaper than you would have done four or five years ago. If I speak to someone in Spain and they say the price is two or three euros, then, if I look at them twice, they'll knock the price down. They're desperate to move stock."

Among Phil's clients are the Brindisa tapas bars, gastropubs, and a number of Spanish restaurants including Cigala, a couple of doors along, of which he is a part owner. He explained that when the wine arrives from Spain, it's delivered to London City Bond, a huge warehouse in Barking. A lorry carrying Albion's wine often contains 1,560 cases, which works out at 18,000 to 19,000 bottles.

He set up Albion Wines thirty years ago, after beginning his career in the wine industry under Peter Dominic in Hereford, during the school holidays. Albion Wines is one of the few surviving independent wine shops left in London. He makes no bones about not being a fan of the large supermarkets, accusing them of being responsible for the demise of wine shops such as Oddbins, Thresher, and Victoria Wine, once familiar names in the high street. "They've wiped out between 3,000 and 4,000 shops!" he complained.

According to Phil, the supermarkets tend to buy from some of the very large producers who are desperate to shift stock. "We tried a selection from a major producer last year and they were not worthy of the name Rioja, quite honestly. They were rubbish!" He reckons you need to spend at least eight or nine pounds if you want a good bottle of wine, and that when supermarkets sell wine for under a fiver it's simply a marketing tool. "But a lot of people don't care what they drink really … Whoever does the week's shopping in the supermarket always ends up going to the booze at the end. And if Tesco is offering 250 bonus points on a wine, they'll buy that."

While supermarkets stock a broad selection of French, Italian, and Australian wines, when it comes to Spanish wine, the selection is more limited. The majority of bottles on the shelves are from La Rioja. Phil has been trying to persuade his customers to explore wines from other regions of Spain, but he admitted it wasn't easy. "We've tried to be innovative in bringing in new wines, new grape varieties and styles, but sometimes it's like banging your head against a brick wall. Rioja is still the big favourite. You can buy wine from Navarra, which is next door to Rioja, and it's the same price. But producers are having terrible problems selling the stuff."

Someone else trying to encourage people to explore Spain's lesser-known wines is José Godoy, sommelier and manager at the restaurant, Ametsa with Arzak Instruction, in Belgravia. In his thirties and dressed in a smart navy blue suit, he has the kind of calm demeanour and easy smile you would expect from someone whose job is to pamper customers in a Michelin-starred restaurant.

José was first introduced to wine when, as a boy, he began helping out at his father's restaurant in Malaga. At the age of twelve he was serving tables and mixing cocktails. He felt at home in restaurants and, by the time he left school, he had worked part-time in several restaurants and hotels in the city, where he began to learn about wine. However, he admitted he got really deeply into it only in 2005, when he did a sommelier course in Marbella while working as a restaurant manager in a top hotel. "I studied eight hours a day for three and a half months. I was very lucky to have the teachers I had. They were full of knowledge and passion."

He joined Ametsa when it opened in 2013, having worked at Calima, a two-Michelin-star restaurant in Marbella run by well-known chef, Dani García. This is his third time in the UK. Previously, he had worked in less glamorous-sounding places: a hotel in the Wirral and a restaurant near Hull.

Spain arrived late on the world wine stage because for a long time it lacked confidence, suggested José. "Spain has an incredible richness in terms of original grapes and varieties but, for some reason, either because of the Spanish personality or history, we never believed it in the same way as the French or Italians did about their wine. In France or Italy, if the wine is not made with original grapes, you can't use a particular appellation. In Spain we always thought foreign grapes were better than ours. Or maybe we thought it was easier to sell a Cabernet Sauvignon or Merlot in the market than Doña Blanca, Verdejo, Albariño and many other Spanish varieties. So now we realise that those Spanish grapes are something unique and give a unique personality to the wines. We are offering something different in the market. There are millions of Cabernet Sauvignon, millions of Syrah. I'm not saying the customers are getting tired of this, but they are keen to discover different things. This is why, now, it's time to open the door to Spanish wines."

At one time, he went on, Spain was fighting over the price of its wines. Now it's fighting for the quality. "We can't compete with Chile or Argentina on price. So our fight has to be with France and Italy in terms of quality."

While José selects wines from across Spain for his customers, he conceded that Rioja will always be the king of Spanish wines. "It represents over thirty per cent of the exports of Spanish wines. And in the wine world it's the brand of Spain. Many customers say, 'I already know Rioja. What else can you offer me?' Or they might say, 'When I drink Rioja, I drink this one. Do you have something similar, or a similar style from a different region?' If someone says to me, 'I don't like Rioja,' I would say, 'Well, Rioja is 300 kilometres wide and has over 1,000 wineries. So you can imagine how many different styles you can find.'"

La Rioja – named after a river, the Rio Oja, which flows into the Ebro – is a region José knows well, having worked in a hotel there. I learned from him that there are three sub-regions in La Rioja, although this isn't always made clear on the labels: Rioja Baja, the flattest and hottest area, which produces Garnacha grapes; Rioja Alavesa, whose chalky clay soil produces Tempranillo; and Rioja Alta, the highest area, located around the town of Haro.

Just what a serious business wine is can be seen in the 2014 annual report of the Rioja DO, which has an annual budget of 14.9 million euros. It runs for seventy-eight pages and contains the kind of bureaucratic detail and statistics you would normally associate with a large financial institution. The report is upbeat about the future of Rioja, pointing out that the 281 million litres of wine produced in 2014 was 5 million up on the previous year.

José revealed that there are rumblings of discontent among some wine producers about the current classification system. In response, there are moves to create sub-appellations by village, estate, and vine-yard, along the lines of the French model. The Catalan region is the only Spanish DO to have established something similar. "The soil changes a lot in different villages, so the producers are realising that you can't have different styles of wine under the same umbrella, be-cause from the customer's point of view it's totally crazy. Sub-appel-lations would make it easier for the customers to identify the wines."

One thing that has always baffled me about wine is how professional tasters are able to distinguish between so many types. For example, there are hundreds if not thousands of red wines out there. Are they really all that distinctive? A few weeks before we met, at *the drinks business* magazine's Rioja Masters 2016, José had done a blind tast-ing of sixty Rioja wines over four hours, and awarded points to each wine. So, to what extent is he able to distinguish between the different wines? Could he tell, for example, which part of a valley grapes were grown on? I've heard some wine experts claim this and I find it very hard to believe. "I can tell the differences between the wines, yes, but not where they are from. Unless you know the producer very well, it's impossible to recognise where the wines are coming from. And to be able to identify a part of a valley, you need to be well trained and to know the area very well."

If some French or Italian reds had been sneaked in among the Riojas, would he have been able to identify them? "Italian wines have a strong personality. If you had a Barolo or Sangiovese, you might be able to tell them. In terms of France, if it was a Burgundy you could tell … and also with Bordeaux, which has a characteristic nose, and because

Cabernet Sauvignon is more tannic than Rioja. I think eighty to ninety per cent I could. There are some modern Riojas which are similar to the Bordeaux style."

When I asked him whether a professional wine taster has a more developed palate than most people, he said it was all to do with memory and training. "Your palate belongs to you and your experience. Everything you smell or taste is within your childhood. There are some aromas which have been in your mind since you were five or six years old. And that's unique to you. If we taste a wine together, you will discover aromas I can't find. And I will discover aromas you can't find."

This made perfect sense to me. For example, every time I smell tarmac, I think of when I used to play on the pavement outside my granny's house in the summer. And every time I smell chrysanthemums, I think of the small church I used to go to as a child. Smells are incredibly powerful and can transport us to somewhere else.

José is spot on when he says that wine professionals need to demystify the world of wine and make it more accessible to ordinary people. "When we are talking among ourselves it's fine to use that vocabulary, but when we are talking to people who are not professionals we need to adapt the vocabulary. Eighty per cent of customers aren't bothered if a wine is made from Tempranillo, Syrah, or Grenache. They are going to drink, enjoy the bottle, and that's it. We need to be able to adapt our skills to people and not think, I'm a professional and you're not. We shouldn't scare people. We need to get people into the wine rather than create a barrier. If people want to get a deeper knowledge of wine, that's fine. But restaurants are not schools. Customers don't come here to learn; they come here to have an experience."

If someone wanted to learn about the wines of Spain, what would be a good starting point? "Rioja", he replied. "I would start with one of each of the three categories, Crianza, Reserva, and Gran Reserva, and try to understand the differences between them." These classifications refer to how long the wine has been aged in oak barrels. There's another type of Rioja, Joven, which hasn't been aged in oak. "At the end of the day, Rioja is the most important wine region in Spain, so you need to know about it. It's like the new chefs starting now. They are probably keen to work with nitrogen, but before they do they need to know what a hollandaise sauce is. You need a base."

I came away with the feeling that this was good advice. Whatever we are interested in, we always need to get a firm grasp of the basics before trying to understand more complex issues.

Over in the City, Dave Green doesn't just want people to drink Spanish wine. He wants them to go and see where it is produced. Dave is the UK director of wines and foods for The Haciendas Company, which produces over fifty million bottles of wine each year from vineyards in many areas of Spain, including Rioja, Ribera del Duero, Rueda, and Arribes del Duero. Customers in the UK account for seven million of these bottles. With brands such as Marqués de la Concordia, Berberana, and Monistrol cava, The Haciendas Company first made inroads into the UK wine market when it started selling to Tesco. It now supplies Sainsbury's, Aldi, and Lidl, along with several pub chains.

"We have done a lot of consumer fairs this year – Spirit of Summer, the Country Living show, and other ones – and the first thing people think of with Spanish wine is Rioja. Then probably cava, then sherry", said Dave, when I met him at Zorita's Kitchen, The Haciendas Company's 130-seater restaurant by the Thames in the wonderfully-named Broken Wharf, a short street between Southwark Bridge and the Millennium Bridge.

"About eighty per cent of sales of Spanish wine are from one grape variety, Tempranillo", he went on. "People are after a certain kind of wine, which they associate with Rioja. Often people will say, 'Oh,

Rioja, I love that grape.' If you have a Tempranillo from a different region, you have to say to people, yes, it's similar to Rioja, it's the same grape varietal and it's aged in oak, but it's from a different region. But now the grape is taking over from the region. We can buy Tempranillo from Extremadura for half the price because Rioja still has that kudos. Actually, the wine that is selling best for us is a Syrah, or Shiraz, from Arribes del Duero, near Salamanca. This is showing an international varietal in a region most people haven't heard of. It's resonated with people because it's dynamic, modern, and quirky."

One of the main ideas behind The Haciendas Company is "farm to table". It wants to take away the mystery about where the food you eat comes from. The ingredients used in the restaurant, and the produce sold in the shop next door, come from its organic farm in Salamanca, where, in a former monastery, it also runs a luxury hotel and spa. Dave said that the company tries to take customers through "stepping stones" to understand Spanish food and how it is produced.

Dave was lured away from Majestic Wine, where he had spent eleven years, to raise the profile of The Haciendas Company in London. It wasn't so much his knowledge of wine that his new employer was after but, because Zorita's Kitchen is located in the City, the contacts he had built up over the years in FTSE 100 companies. The business also operates restaurants in Madrid and Stavanger, in Norway, and has hired Victor Gutierrez, a Michelin-starred chef from Salamanca, as an adviser. But, when it opened in London in 2007, its farm to table idea was slow to catch on. Back then, the business occupied only the ground floor of its current premises and was limited to running the shop and providing food tastings and wine pairings. Dave reckons they have done nearly 700 tastings.

Many diners in the City now find this farm to table idea appealing, perhaps not just because it's seen as a way of connecting to more natural food, but because it has connotations of a less stressful and fast-paced life. Dave told me he expects 36,000 people through the doors this year and that, that evening, a group of forty will be arriving to taste the ham and seven wines. "Eighty-three per cent of our customers are City workers. They use the restaurant in three ways: entertaining clients, going out with colleagues or friends, and networking. In terms of tourists and residents, we get a few at weekends. But this isn't who we are trying to reach out to."

Dave talked enthusiastically about "experiential marketing", meaning that he wants to raise awareness of the company's products rather than just build a big business. "You go into the restaurant and order from the menu and then what we want you to do is recreate that menu at home. Almost everything on our menu is available for purchase in our shop." He added that there are a lot more Spanish people working in London recently, and often they dine out at high-end Spanish restaurants as a way of showing clients how proud they are of their country.

The Haciendas Company has cashed in on the growing interest in the gastronomy of Spain by providing short breaks at its farm and hotel in Salamanca. Guests can see the wine being made, take a balloon flight over the Duero Valley, visit the organic farm to take part in a cheese tasting, and go to Salamanca and do a tour of its restaurants. Most of those who book are what Dave calls "empty nesters", people aged fifty-five to sixty-five whose children have graduated from university. And nearly 250 customers have paid to join the membership club, enticed by a free quarterly case of wine, a free night's stay in the hotel, and invitations to wine tastings."

Dave stressed that Spain is still the top tourist destination for British people. "I think that as Spain has opened up with its transport links getting a lot better ... people are exploring a lot more. Traditionally, people went to the coast, but now they are looking for other things, such as all the World Heritage Sites. And then they want to recreate the experience at home or go and find it in their local town or city. We've looked at all the tourism stats to see if people have changed from the bucket and spade approach to Spain, and I think they have, especially the higher socio-economic group but also the age range we are looking at, which is looking for more of an educational than an activity holiday. The people who stay at our hotel come back to the UK and become our ambassadors. They sell the company for us."

Sherry has made a big comeback. So that I could learn more about the attractions of this drink, Richard Bigg of Camino had invited me to attend a sherry tasting session with some of his staff at the premises in Mincing Lane, a narrow street of office blocks near Fenchurch Street Station. It was the middle of the afternoon and the only customers were a group of office workers who seemed to be enjoying a very long and, in the case of one man, extremely loud lunch. The chefs were busy in the open kitchen, preparing for the early evening crowd who would be coming through the doors in a couple of hours.

I sat at the end of several tables pushed together beneath a large wall map of Spain. Most of the sixteen waiters, waitresses, and bar staff were in their early- to mid-twenties, and there was the kind of giggly atmosphere you find at school on the last day of term. As we waited for Master of Wine, Peter McCombie, to begin, I worried about what the effects might be of tasting six sherries at this time of day, especially as I had to attend an olive oil tasting session at a *jamón* bar later on.

Peter, an imposing and engaging Kiwi in his fifties, kicked off by pointing to the map and explaining that three towns in Andalusia, Jerez de la Frontera, Sanlúcar de Barrameda, and El Puerto de Santa María, form what is known as the "sherry triangle". He said that sherry comes in two broad styles: pale ones, which are dry, and darker ones, which are sweet. The main grape used is Palomino but, unlike with wine, that's not what makes it interesting; it's the ageing process that does this.

One of the managers got up and brought back a bottle of La Goya Manzanilla and went around the table, pouring a small amount into each of our glasses.

"The first thing you do is look at the glass, then you smell it", said Peter, pushing his nose into the glass. "When you smell, what you are doing is saying, 'Is this good enough to put in my mouth?' Because we don't put things in our mouths that smell bad, do we?"

As Peter must have intended, this last comment produced laughter from some of the staff.

"Is it clean? Fresh? Is it good?" he continued. "The next thing we do is the swirly thing. The swirly thing is really just to release the aromatic elements in the wine, so that they become easier to smell. I've been doing this for a long time, but I still manage to spill it down my shirt. So you can place it on the table and swirl it if you want." I joined the staff in smelling the sherry.

"What do you smell?" asked Peter, strolling casually along the table.

Bread, suggested a waitress. Citrus, ventured someone else. Almonds, piped up another voice.

"It smells like being on a beach", said Peter. "You know when you are by a rock pool on a windy day?" I could see by the expressions on the faces around me that I wasn't the only one taken aback by this novel suggestion.

"You might think this is bullshit", said Peter. "You don't have to agree, but maybe I like the poetry of that and I know this is matured by the sea. Salt is a physical taste. You can't smell it. But I want to say it smells salty." He instructed us to put a small amount of wine in our mouths and not to swallow it, but rather move it around with our tongues to warm it up so that we got more flavour. This was a very dry sherry that went with salty flavours. "It makes my juices flow and I want to eat. I've sat drinking it on the waterfront at Sanlúcar with a plate of prawns and garlic and I was in heaven. But in a bar, maybe you would have salted almonds, olives, or *boquerones*."

Despite Peter's lavish praise, I wasn't keen on the sherry. It tasted a little bitter, and I was relieved when the staff around me began tipping their glasses into a metal container on the table. However, I was totally captivated by Peter's brilliant poetic descriptions. He could have had an equally successful career dreaming up advertising slogans.

The point of the tasting, he emphasised, is to try and work out why you prefer one sherry to another. "When it comes to wine, make up your own mind. If you don't like it, ask yourself why."

After tasting Tio Pepe Fino, which to me was indistinguishable from the first one, we tried the Amontillado Viña AB. Peter informed us that it had been aged for eleven years and had sixteen and a half per cent alcohol by volume. He sniffed the glass. "It seems quite spicy and reminds me of old churches." One of the staff said brightly that it reminded him of wood. Peter nodded, sniffed again, paused and said, "Yeah, it smells like rotten leaves … or being in a wood in autumn."

When we sniffed an Oloroso Classic, Peter declared that the aroma was of roasted walnuts or hazelnuts. Someone at the far end of the table called out that it smelled of polish. Peter shook his head. "Shoe polish probably isn't a good word to use when describing the wine to customers." He advised saying that it smelled like burning leaves on a bonfire. The assistant manager called out that it reminded him of when you drive a car into a garage. "Benzine!" came back Peter. "Yes, that's it, Benzine!" called out the assistant manager.

Peter explained that this sherry works well with hard cheese. "Maybe someone would like to finish off with a glass of it at the end of the evening. But it's not about being pushy with customers. It's about making an offer."

The next sherry, Solera 1847 Oloroso Dulce, which Peter thought smelled like raisins or dry figs, was delicious, far sweeter than the others. "You could sell this to someone as a dessert", he said. "You could serve it on the rocks. If someone wants it on the rocks, why not?"

But the final sherry, Nectar Pedro Ximenez, was even more delicious, and tasted even sweeter. One of the staff thought the aroma was like Christmas pudding, another suggested coffee. I agreed and thought I could detect caramel. Peter loved the Christmas pudding comparison and suggested that there was a hint of orange peel too. He then revealed that it contained a whopping 350 grammes of sugar in every litre. "The thing is," he grinned, "you don't need to share that number with the customers."

If a customer says they don't like sherry, the staff should ask which kind of sherry and explain there are many different styles, urged Peter. It's all about giving people a chance to try things. If a customer wants a cheaper glass of wine and they enjoy it, it makes good business sense because they've had a good experience and will leave happy.

When it comes to taste, Peter believes there are three groups of people. At one end are those he calls "hyper tasters", people who have a heightened sense of taste and are often fussier about what they eat or drink. At the other end of the spectrum are those he calls "non tasters", who don't seem to care too much what they eat. Chefs and others who are professionally involved with food tend to be in the middle. I liked the model Peter presented, but I wasn't sure which category I fitted into. I cared about what I ate, but I didn't consider myself to have an exceptional sense of taste. And I wasn't a chef.

When I left Camino and headed across London Bridge to go to the olive oil tasting session, I felt grateful to Peter for explaining sherry in such a wonderfully entertaining way. His message seemed to be, don't worry if you don't know that much about wine or aren't able to describe it. Just find a wine that you like to drink and enjoy it. However, I wasn't sure if I would ever understand how certain wines go well with some types of food. But maybe that's not really necessary. As Will Lyons, wine writer in *The Dish*, The *Sunday Times*'s food magazine, says, "Think of the wine as an ingredient, a spice or a dressing, something that will add to the flavour and enjoyment of the meal, but won't overwhelm it."

Malcolm Gluck, in *The Great Wine Swindle*, has a very different, more controversial, message. He maintains that, when it comes to wine, we are all being conned. "Wine is the only everyday product which most of its users believe so complex that one must pass an advanced driving test in order to steer one's way through it." His advice echoes that of Peter: just drink the wine you like and don't worry if you don't know all the technical stuff.

This is certainly what Antonio Docampo García from Vigo in Galicia did. Before his death in 2015, at the age of 107, he claimed his longevity was down to him drinking four bottles of homemade wine each day, and never touching water.

Just how varied Spanish wine is became apparent when I attended the 2016 Wines from Spain trade fair at Tobacco Dock, a former nineteenth-century warehouse near Tower Bridge. Over forty importers had booked stands, along with twenty Spanish wineries, and bottles of wine from hundreds of *bodegas* stood invitingly on the tables. I spent a pleasant couple of hours tasting what was on offer and, as I had to collect my son from school that afternoon, remembering to empty most of the contents of each glass into the metal bowls provided.

I spoke to several exporters who were hoping to find an importer to sell their wine in the UK. Many were already selling to Germany, Italy, Japan, and elsewhere. They told me about the grapes they used, the climate and soil in their region, and the origins of their family-run *bodegas*. One woman from a company in La Rioja explained that there were eighty *bodegas* near her village.

"Does everyone drink Rioja when they go to a bar?" I asked, aware that beer was more popular than wine in Spain.

"Yes. We are very proud of it. You know, in Spain we are very attached to where we come from", she replied.

At the stand of a company from Castilla-La Mancha, I discovered that some of the wines had been named after members of the family, which I thought was a nice touch. A Belgian guy from the charmingly-named Spanish Story in Madrid was promoting wines from five DOs, made with seven varieties of grapes. He explained how his company had decided to create a series of very colourful eye-catching labels, each in the same style and each containing a different image: a pig, a bull, a shrimp, an octopus. I thought it was a brilliant idea. The labels were attractive and really stood out.

When I mentioned to several of the exporters that I was writing a book about Spanish food and wine, I had expected a lively discussion about eating and drinking in London, but instead received blank expressions. I was surprised by this. It made me wonder how much thought the exporters had given to the London market and what might make it unique. According to the owner of one wine shop, the UK market was unlike other European markets because of the variety of wine from around the world on offer. "You won't get such choice in France, Italy, or many other countries in Europe", he told me. Nevertheless, I got the impression that the exporters who had turned up to Wines from Spain appeared to be focussed only on what they were producing. I felt that, if they want to break into the UK market, they need to focus more on what their potential UK customers might want, and what they might pay for it.

6. A Shrine to Jamón

"In the north they don't need to add much salt to ham, while in the south they need to."

Noelia Rojilla, Bar Tozino

The bull might be the animal most associated with Spain, but it's the pig that Spaniards really love. When Noelia Rojilla, the chef at Bar Tozino, talks about ham, it's as if the fate of the world depends on it. To someone British, getting so excited about ham might sound a little strange. If we buy some ham at our local butcher or supermarket, we just think of it as something to put in a sandwich. But in Spain, ham is revered, and you find it in every bar and restaurant.

Situated in a railway arch off Maltby Street in the back streets of Bermondsey, just a short walk from Tower Bridge, Bar Tozino claims to be London's first *jamón* bar. A review in *Harper's Magazine* described it as "a hidden gem that has quietly found a following – especially for those who love great tapas and sherry."

The idea that Bermondsey would become a foodie destination was unthinkable when I lived there in the early 1980s. In those days it was a poorly lit area of sprawling council estates, small fried egg and bacon cafés, and pubs where Millwall football fans would congregate on Saturday afternoons. I remember the air was always filled with the smells of chocolate and vinegar from the Peek Frean and Sarson's factories and, if you wandered past the abandoned warehouses, you could still detect the faint smells of ginger and cinnamon.

Today, the factories have been turned into business complexes, and the warehouses by the river have become expensive flats with gyms and stylish restaurants below, while modern apartment blocks flank the railway lines flowing into London Bridge station. Most of those dodgy pubs have closed, and branches of Tesco Express and Sainsbury's Local have opened up to meet the needs of the City types who arrive back late in the evening in fleets of black cabs. With the Jubilee Line now whizzing you to Oxford Street or Canary Wharf in less than fifteen minutes, it's easy to see why Bermondsey is popular. The prediction an estate agent made some years ago that Bermondsey would become the Mayfair of south London wasn't that far off.

Small and dark, Bar Tozino reminded me of a cave. With its hams hanging from the ceiling, and the old wooden and brick walls, you could easily imagine a group of Spanish farm workers in thick boots chatting animatedly to each other, while putting slices of wafer thin ham into their mouths between sips of cold sherry. Noelia, a petite and bubbly twenty-nine-year old, told me that the arch is ideal for hanging hams, as it's like a cellar, and that, because the hams are cured, there are no problems with flies, something the health inspectors didn't initially believe. She invited me to try each of the five ham legs sitting on the bar in *jamonero* stands.

"What do you think?" she asked, cutting a thin sliver off one of them and holding the knife out to me.

"Mm, it's got a salty flavour", I said, as the ham dissolved in my mouth.

"You like it?"

"Yes."

"Try this one", she said, cutting a piece from a different ham.

"Mm. This doesn't taste quite as salty."

"It's from Salamanca. In the north they don't need to add much salt to ham, while in the south they do."

The reverence with which Noelia approached each of the hams reminded me of the episode of Rick Stein's programme when he visited a ham factory in a small town near the border with Portugal. He was met by the popular London chef, José Pizarro, who told him, as they climbed the stairs to the rooms where the hams were hung, "It's a place very close to heaven." Stein replied that it was like a cathedral of ham. This religious theme was further developed when the ham carver, dressed in what resembled white vestments and a colourful stole, carefully cut some slices. "People watch this in silence", said another worker reverently. "It's like when you are in a church and the priest consecrates the bread and wine."

If that ham factory Stein visited was a cathedral to ham, then Bar Tozino was a shrine. Yet, to be honest, I couldn't tell much difference between the different hams. Yes, some were a little saltier or nuttier than others, but they all tasted very similar. I wasn't sure if this was because my palate isn't that finely tuned, or because the Spanish sometimes go over the top when they talk about their produce. Whichever it was, I didn't say this to Noelia.

Spanish ham can seem confusing. Given the importance of it in Spanish gastronomy, its production is subject to strict regulations, covering the breed of pigs and what they are fed on. In 2015, the Spanish Embassy in London held an event to explain to restaurant owners and chefs the new quality standards governing Ibérico ham. From now on, ham would be graded by four coloured labels: black (one-hundred per cent acorn-fed Ibérico), red (partly acorn-fed), green (countryside fodder-fed), and white (fodder-fed).

As I had discovered when I met my friend, Curro, at his ham factory on the border between Extremadura and Andalusia, Ibérico and Ibérico de Bellota (*bellota* means acorn) are produced on the west side of Spain, in an area stretching from Castilla y León in the north down through Extremadura to Andalusia in the south. Serrano (meaning from the mountains) ham, on the other hand, is more commonly found in the east, particularly around Teruel in Aragón, and comes from the white pigs that you find across Europe.

Ibérico and Ibérico de Bellota ham come from what are known as the black pigs, because of their black hooves, and which are found only in Spain. The pigs roam freely out in the *dehesa*, the vast areas of land in western Spain punctuated by dark green oak and cork trees.

From October to March, some of the pigs eat only acorns, which makes them very fat. After this, they are slaughtered, something that used to be done at home in many villages in Spain. It's the acorns that give the Ibérico de Bellota a distinctive nutty flavour. The acorns are rich in oleic acid, which is also produced by olives, making the ham moist and sweet.

The curing process for Ibérico hams can be as long as three years. That, and the fact that the pigs are rarer (they account for only ten per cent of pigs in Spain), explain why the ham costs much more than Serrano. And Spaniards don't waste anything from the pig. Curro's shop at the factory sold *morcilla* (like black pudding), *chorizo*, *salchichón* (like salami), and other meat products.

In Bar Tozino, Noelia told me, "They are going to get rid of the words '*patra negra*'."

"Why?" I asked.

"Because some people have painted the feet of white pigs black."

"Really?"

"Yeah, it's true, so they can say it's Ibérico ham."

With so much money to be made from Ibérico ham, it was perhaps not surprising that there were some unscrupulous producers.

After I tasted the ham, Noelia announced that she was going to cook a *chorizo* and chick pea stew. She was doing this purely for my benefit.

When I first met her a few weeks earlier at the olive oil tasting session, and asked if I could return and interview her, she had suggested that I come and watch her cook one afternoon when Bar Tozino was closed. Not every chef would be willing to do this.

I perched myself on a wooden stool at the bar and watched as she began to slice some long *chorizo* sausages into small chunks. She was using a *chorizo* called *chistorra* from Navarra. It was so soft it almost crumbled like Cheshire cheese when she ran the knife through it.

"The *chistorra* is thinner than the *chorizo* I usually cook with. But I like it", she said.

It felt odd sitting in an empty bar. It was the silence I noticed the most: bars are usually filled with noise. It was so quiet that it was indeed like being inside a small chapel.

"We are going to put it with some garlic, onion, and herbs – rosemary, bay leaves, and sage", she said, picking up a pan.

"OK", I replied, feeling like a pupil at school.

"We are going to cook it and then we add wine, a little bit of *pimentón*, and some chick peas", she continued.

I felt admiration at the way chefs know exactly what ingredients to put in a dish, when to put them in, and in what amounts. I've always regarded them as a little bit like magicians. If you're cooking at home, it can be a tense experience as you hover over the cooker and doubts soon seep in. Did I put too much of that in? Did I boil it long enough? Have I added too much salt? We home cooks usually have the enthusiasm and passion, but most of the time not the technical knowledge, skills, or – just as important – intuition.

Noelia's kitchen occupies one side behind the bar, so the customers can see everything that goes on. It doesn't contain much more than two rings, an eighteen-inch oven, a toaster, and a sink. Because the kitchen is so small, she says it can take a lot of time to prepare dishes for any of the large events for which Bar Tozino provides the food. Also, she can't cook seafood much because it makes the kitchen too smoky. She's devised a short menu that she knows she can deliver even when the bar is packed and orders are flying at her one after the other.

"On Saturdays we serve a plate of food every thirty seconds!" she explained.

"Every thirty seconds?" I said, staggered by this piece of information. Talk about fast food.

"Oh, yeah. In general, we have ninety covers. One time we had 254. It was crazy!" she said, her voice rising, as if she couldn't quite believe she had cooked for so many people. On Saturdays, she'll often make as many as eight or nine *tortillas*.

"I feel confident cooking at home for five or six friends, but I couldn't imagine cooking for dozens of people", I said. She nodded in recognition. "If you can cook for your family and friends at home, then it just comes down to organisation. At the beginning, I was cooking for fifty people, then two-hundred, and then a thousand at a festival."

This made sense. Cooking, like many things in life, is partly about confidence. At one time, the thought of cooking for half a dozen people would have petrified me. But now I can take it in my stride. Well, more or less. But two-hundred people!

I asked why some *chorizo* you buy in the shops is hard and some is soft. The hard *chorizo* is cured, she explained, so you can eat it with bread, say. The soft *chorizo*, on the other hand, has to be cooked. "Afterwards I remove a little bit of the oil from the pan, because it gets very heavy on the stomach and I think Spanish food is already quite rich."

Fetching a double electric ring, she switched it on and then put a small saucepan on one of the rings before pouring a drop of olive oil in. She tipped in some onions she had caramelised earlier, followed by the garlic and the *chorizo*. "I like cooking in little pans because it's like cooking at home. It's very relaxing."

"You're cooking on a low heat", I said.

"I discovered that if I cook on a higher heat, the *chorizo* gets brown on the outside but is chewy inside, because the fat doesn't melt properly. Once it has cooked I can put the heat higher. This is how I like it. I don't know if this is the right way or not, but it's something I do."

Noelia didn't take the traditional route to becoming a chef. Back home in Madrid, she did a variety of jobs – bingo caller, waitress, sales assistant, running a rehab programme in a prison – before coming to London in 2007 on an internship linked to her psychology degree, to learn English. "If I had stayed in Spain, I don't think I would have ended up cooking professionally."

She left Spain when it was on the verge of its biggest economic crisis in recent years, which resulted in soaring rates of unemployment, especially among the young, as well as a collapse in the property market and meltdown in the construction industry.

As with most chefs, food was a dominant theme in Noelia's childhood. Although her mum was a good cook, she didn't have much time to spend in the kitchen. When her parents were at work, Noelia and her sister would go to the market together, buy some food and then go home and cook it. "I think it was more about seeing the ingredients in the market that made me want to cook."

When she came to London, she got a job selling spiced lamb, chicken tagine, and marinated pork on a stall in Exmouth Market. She struck lucky, because the stall was run by Moro, a restaurant that has received glowing reviews from food critics for its North African food. Its sister restaurant Morito, also in Exmouth Market, serves Spanish cuisine and has received equally outstanding reviews. She was soon asked to help out in the kitchen at Moro, which is where she really learned how to cook properly. "I was sometimes preparing ninety kilograms of lamb and twenty kilograms of houmous. At the beginning, I thought this was impossible. Some of the most important things I learned were that you need to take your work in the kitchen very seriously, like how to use spices, and you must be organised."

Bar Tozino started out as a stall selling ham in Maltby Street Market, which began by the railway arches in 2009 when Monmouth Coffee opened up there. Other food producers, some of whom had run stalls at nearby Borough Market, soon followed.

Noelia worked on the stall in Maltby Street with her boyfriend Zac Fingal Rock-Innes, a Welshman, and Chuse Valero, who had both worked at Brindisa. Chuse had also been a ham carver in Barcelona. The stall proved to be very popular and, in 2012, they took on a lease at a railway arch in Ropewalk and opened Bar Tozino.

"In the beginning, we just opened on Saturdays, then on Saturdays and Sundays, then on Fridays, Saturdays, and Sundays. We didn't expect to do so well", reflected Noelia, tipping the herbs into the pan, and explaining that they give more flavour when added at the beginning.

So how much has Bar Tozino changed since it opened?

"I saw the first menu the other day and it was just ham, Manchego cheese, and red and white wine. That was it."

The stew had been cooking now for about fifteen minutes and, with the herbs now going to work, it smelled fantastic. "I cook by eye. I never check the time. I think that you can see how things are and you can taste at the end. Maybe later I add some salt. I know some chefs take three grammes of this and cook for fifteen minutes … but it's more instinctive for me", she said, to the sound of another train rumbling overhead.

To add additional flavour, she added small pieces of hard ham from the leg and, because it contains marrow, a piece of ham on the bone.

She said that she was in her teens when she first began to understand how different flavours worked together. Meeting Zac expanded her knowledge further.

She poured a glass of Conde Valdemar, a white wine from La Rioja, into the pan. She said that red wine, which is often used with meat, is too acidic for the stew. Then she added two teaspoons of *pimentón* and the chick peas and brought everything to the boil, explaining that this would help the flavours come together.

When the stew was ready, she spooned it into two small dishes, saying that she adapted the recipe from the *cocido* (a chick pea-based stew) she ate in Madrid. "The people love it and I like it a lot. But for me it's not *cocido*."

I dug my spoon into the stew. It might not have been the *cocido* that Noelia was familiar with, but it was delicious, packed with flavour and the tang of rosemary. It was the kind of hearty, filling food you want to eat in the winter.

Pointing to a large black pot that looked like a beer barrel, she said that she made three soup kettles of the stew each week. "I know that the soup kettle can provide twenty-six portions. You know, in a kitchen you have to know how to control and count everything."

Tozino had been part of Tapas Fantasticas, a road show promoting Rioja wine and Spanish food in Britain and Ireland, and she had taken her soup kettle to Dublin, Edinburgh, and Bristol, and would soon be going to Oxford. In Bristol, she had served 1,000 portions of her chick pea and *chorizo* stew.

Despite all the hard work involved, she enjoys cooking at the festivals because it gives her an opportunity to introduce Spanish dishes to people who might not have tried them before. "In Dublin, the sales were good but maybe people didn't understand the concept. It's nice to make money but it's also nice for people to understand the concept. In

Bristol, we didn't make much more money but the people were more interested."

But cooking single-handedly in a small bar, or at a festival, can take its toll, she conceded, saying that she became so stressed with it all last year that she went away for a while, to learn how to meditate.

After we finished the stew, she jumped up and said she was going to make *migas*, running upstairs to the storeroom and returning with a plastic container of breadcrumbs. She said she began making *migas* when she found that she had left-over bread. It's now become one of the bestsellers on the menu. It's a dish I had never tried, but I remembered Rick Stein, in his series, meeting a man who cooked *migas* in a pot over an open fire in his shed, under a bridge in Trujillo in Extremadura. He had made it with strips of belly pork, peppers, *chorizo*, and garlic, and topped it off with breadcrumbs.

"Basically, *migas* is a dish the shepherds used to eat. Some people add *chorizo*, some people peppers, some people sardines. It depends on the area. So there's not one way to make *migas*", Noelia said, adding that the breadcrumbs are soaked in water before being fried, to make them softer. She showed me a pan containing fried *chorizo*, pancetta, pieces of the hard ham, garlic, and onion, and said she would mix this with the breadcrumbs when they were fried.

The *migas* reminded me of eating an English fry-up. I could see why it's popular at Tozino, especially if you're a bit hung over from the night before. It was comforting and satisfying food.

According to Noelia, there's a difference between the food you would eat at a typical restaurant in Spain and the Spanish food being served in London. "For example, you can't find a simple dish like *patatas bravas* in London. It's one of my favourite dishes. In fact, the original sauce shouldn't have tomatoes."

"No?"

"No! It should have just *pimentón* and onion with oil. With tomatoes is nice, but it's not the original. To be honest, I'm also upset with the *bravas* in some places in Spain."

I mentioned that I had just returned from holidays in Granada and Malaga and that I hadn't seen much evidence of fast food outlets such as Burger King and McDonald's. She suggested that students sometimes like them, but that most people would rather buy a *bocadillo* (sandwich roll), which generally costs about two euros. In fact, I later discovered, McDonald's has over 400 restaurants in Spain. Despite its wonderful food, it appears that Spain, too, might be gradually succumbing to fast food culture.

Looking to the future of Spanish restaurants in London, she suggested that restaurants might market themselves as, for example, Galician, or Basque.

"Something that I think will work in London at some point is the *asador*, where you have big pieces of roasted meat, like suckling pig. The place has a big charcoal grill and big ovens. The meat is cut with a plate."

"A plate?" I wasn't sure I'd heard her correctly.

"Yeah", she said, laughing, and scrolled through the photos on her iPhone to show me a picture of someone cutting suckling pig with a white plate. "It's very soft. I think part of the Spanish gastronomic culture will work in London. It's part of the show. It's like a Japanese chef cooking in front of you. It's nice."

Bar Tozino has moved into wholesaling, and has become so popular that it is hoping to take over the adjacent railway arch and hold ham carving classes and wine tastings.

"When we opened the bar we didn't have any money, so we had to work very hard. Now I'm training people so that I am able to do other things in the company", she said.

If Bar Tozino expands, it will mean that Noelia will have more space in which to cook. This is, she admitted, something she can't wait for.

7. The Pioneer

"Fifty years ago, Spain was almost as undiscovered as Africa."

Monika Linton, Brindisa

It was a Spanish sheep's milk cheese in a tin from Castilla y León that dramatically changed Monika Linton's career. Had she not discovered it, she might still be standing at the front of a classroom, teaching foreign students about the difference between a preposition and a conjunction. Instead, she's in charge of Brindisa, the company that has blazed a trail in bringing top quality Spanish produce to London since she started it nearly thirty years ago. It now operates five restaurants and two shops, and is a major wholesaler. And it has done something unthinkable for a British company: open a restaurant in Spain.

"That cheese, which was in extra virgin olive oil and in a tin, won the hearts of the people who tried it because the flavour was so incredible", Monika told me when I met her one afternoon at Brindisa's shop and café, situated in one of the railway arches along Atlantic Road in Brixton. "It wasn't called Manchego and it wasn't conventional and the taste was outrageously good", she continued. "So some of the chefs in London fell in love with it. They had never tasted anything like it."

The chances are that if people were asked to name some Spanish cheeses, one in particular would come up: Manchego. Yet Spain produces over a hundred types of cheese, made from cow's milk, sheep's milk, goat's milk, or combinations of these.

Tall, with long auburn hair, and wearing jeans, desert boots, and a colourful scarf around her neck, Monika speaks in one of those Home

Counties accents that tell you she was educated at a posh school. The Brindisa café doesn't open in the afternoons, as there's not enough demand for it yet, so Monika and I are sitting there alone. I can hear a chef banging pots and pans about in the kitchen as he prepares for the customers who will start arriving again at five o'clock. There is still something of the English teacher about her and, sitting across the table from her in the empty room, I briefly imagine discussing with her an essay I've written: "That's a good observation about Shylock, but perhaps you could expand it a bit more."

Brixton is a part of south-west London that always seems to be pumping with energy, just as it always seems to have a river of red double-decker buses trickling through the high street. Over the years, it's often been in the news for the wrong reasons, notably street crime and gangs. Nevertheless, there are few areas of London that can match it for sheer colour and vitality. Reggae music blares from the covered market, Pentecostal preachers with megaphones stand outside the Tube station urging you to repent, and Muslims offer you leaflets about the Koran. Along Stockwell Road, small Portuguese cafés cluster, while, in the piazza in front of the Ritzy cinema, smiling Rastas high-five each other when they meet.

In the last few years, though, as in Bermondsey and Peckham, gentrification has been radically changing the area. Trendy bars and restaurants have opened and John Lewis delivery vans can be seen driving slowly along the streets of Victorian terrace houses. Understandably, not everyone is happy with the changes taking place, but it could be argued that Brixton is returning to what it was in the nineteenth century, a prosperous middle-class suburb.

One of the reasons Monika chose Brixton for her second shop is that she lives close by, near Brockwell Park, with her husband and two teenage children. The other is that she likes the idea of being close to a market. "The cultural mix is really brilliant and fits with our food. Latin Americans recognise a lot of the ingredients that we sell and a lot of our food is the kind you can take for picnics in the park when it's hot and sunny. The shop really suits the area."

Being a local, she shares some of the concerns others have expressed about the way the retail landscape in Brixton has changed. "There are fewer food retailers in the market. There are now more and more places to eat rather than places to shop. All the residential building going on will further change the area. Property prices have gone up in London a lot, but around here they seem to be going up faster. It feels like it's just been discovered. But the problem with gentrification is that you risk alienating a lot of people that give the place its soul."

Brindisa's shop and café, with its hams and dried red peppers hanging in the large window, looks slightly out of place among the shops selling plastic buckets and storage boxes, cheap meat and fish, vegetables, and hair extensions and cosmetics. But around the corner in the indoor market is Brixton Village, where, at weekends, Bugaboo families, hipsters, and girls in vintage skirts sit around tables eating rare breed beef burgers and drinking craft beer, before, perhaps, picking up a bag of salted caramel brownies on their way home.

But back to how cheese changed Monika's life. Once that sheep's milk cheese in a tin had started to open doors for her, she began importing other cheeses, such as Idiazabal, Mahón, Ibores, and the famous Manchego. Through cold calling and, no doubt, her charm, she managed to persuade Selfridges and Fortnum & Mason to buy from her. "At the time, there was no competition when it came to importing cheese from Spain. I tried to convince the shops that Spanish cheese was as important as cheese from France or Italy and that, as Spain was about to join the EU, they should be stocking it."

However, she soon learned that, financially, Spanish cheese wasn't viable back then. "It's hard selling expensive cheese to people. The majority of people find it difficult to even spend money on a proper artisan Manchego, let alone a super cheese from a special breed in a special tin with olive oil. A lot of people just buy standard mild cheddar. By selling artisan cheese your public is reduced automatically."

The Brindisa story begins not in Brixton but in Monika's cosmopolitan and itinerant childhood. She was born in Malawi, where her parents first met, and part of her childhood was spent living in Africa and the Far East. Unlike some expats, her parents believed in the importance of integrating with the local community in which they lived. As a child, Monika was taken around local markets by her mother. "We got used to enjoying other countries and other foods and we met people who knew about their country's ingredients and cooking traditions. This made food very interesting for me. Food in my childhood wasn't just about the Sunday roast. We had Sunday roasts, but we also ate the local dishes in the countries where we lived."

One of her earliest memories is of the curry lunches her mum prepared on Sundays at their house in Lagos. Monika would put tomatoes, pineapple, coconut, bananas, peanuts, and mango on the Lazy Susan, a circular tray that rotated on the table. Friends would turn up and they would all sit around a table outside on the patio, eating and chatting in the shade until the sun went down over the palm trees that ringed the garden.

Her father's colourful stories of his travels around Spain when he was a student excited her imagination. "Fifty years ago, Spain was almost as undiscovered as Africa. Those stories stuck in my mind." In those days, Spain was still under the grip of Franco and isolated from the rest of Europe. In her book, *Spain*, Jan Morris described the Spain she encountered in the early 1960s as like an island. "Whichever way you enter her … instantly you feel a sense of separateness – a geographical fact exaggerated by historical circumstance."

Things were beginning to change, though, especially on the Mediterranean coastline. In *The New Spaniards*, John Hooper points out that, between 1959 and 1973, the number of visitors to Spain shot up from under three million to over thirty-four million per year.

While the romantic and exotic tales told by Monika's father played a part in her choosing to study Spanish at University College London, her Spanish teacher at New Hall Convent, a Catholic boarding school in Essex, also inspired her. "I was lucky to have Mrs Bosley, who came from Valencia. She was an excellent teacher, and because her A-level classes had only five or six students, you got a lot of attention. She would often bring in Spanish books. I can still remember *El Camino* by Miguel Delibes for my Spanish O-level. It was a story about a small boy with big eyes like an owl, who lived in a village … and I'm sure there was a donkey in it."

After university, she went to Spain for a holiday and ended up doing a TEFL (Teaching English as a foreign language) course in Barcelona, spending the next three years as an English teacher. But it was the couple of months helping out in a restaurant on the Costa Brava that made the biggest impression on her. "I worked in the kitchen, making puddings and salads and things, surrounded by very good cooking. It left a mark on me, because although the teaching was fine, it wasn't something I wanted to do forever. The experience in the restaurant, and then living in a rural part of Spain as a teacher, gave me an interest in the food."

When she returned to England in the mid-1980s, she wanted to find a job that would enable her to use Spanish, and ended up teaching foreign students in language schools. "There weren't that many options. I could have been a bilingual secretary, but I didn't want to do that. I tried to get a job with Amnesty and VSO (Voluntary Services Overseas) in South America, but nothing came of it."

Her brother was working in the City, but he got tired of the corporate world and wanted to do something entrepreneurial. So he quit and moved to Barcelona, where he started selling Stilton cheese and Scottish smoked salmon. Monika got involved when he decided to bring back cheese and wine to the UK and, in 1988, with a friend, they set up Brindisa as a limited company.

Few people in Britain knew anything about Spanish food in those days, she mused. "The kind of British people who went to Provence or Tuscany might also go to Spain. Very few people knew about Spanish food. My aim was to try and get Spanish food accepted by the British and to be understood. Everyone knew about Paris fashion and Italian food but Spain didn't really have any appeal at the time. It was where we went for beach holidays and drank *sangria*, and it was all pretty tacky. Spain was cheap, so if you came with the most expensive Spanish ham or cheese to the British they wouldn't buy it. What we had to do was show British people that Spain wasn't just about beaches and that it had a lot of people in the middle who made amazing food."

Before importing cheese from Spain, she had tried selling Spanish wine. With bottles in a carrier bag, she would turn up at wine merchants and try to persuade them to buy from her. Most weren't interested. Although she sold a few bottles to friends of her parents, her wine career never really took off, she admitted. "I probably sold about three pallets. It was really slow work. I didn't know much about grape varietals, ageing, or any of the other things that are important with wine. If you really didn't know your stuff you were a nobody. It wasn't for me."

Being a woman must have made it harder, I said.

"Absolutely. It was very male dominated. I don't think I was taken very seriously. I think loving wine is one thing, but trying to sell it, and being in the wine industry, is totally different.

An Enterprise Allowance grant, introduced by Margaret Thatcher's government to help people set up small businesses, enabled Monika to work and also receive a small payment, the equivalent to unemployment benefit, each week. Perhaps more importantly, it also meant that she could attend free courses in book-keeping, accountancy, marketing, and other key elements in understanding how to run a business.

When she began importing Spanish cheese, rather than rent a premises she worked from her parents' house in Hampshire, storing her products in the local milkman's fridge and with other local food companies. "I'd say, 'Have you got a corner where I could put some cheese?' I also used all their logistics, I didn't need a driver or anything. I didn't want any fixed overheads. Fixed overheads are a killer."

Sensing a growing interest in Spanish food, she started to import *pimentón*, *chorizo*, Ibérico ham, and other products. She began to realise that she was on to a winner when chefs at Spanish restaurants would speak to her when she phoned. "When I called people and they didn't buy from me, I would still keep in touch with them. I think they thought, 'Mm, she's a persistent person, there must be something in it.' They would say, give me a call in two months' time, and that's what I would do." One of those chefs was José Pizarro, who went on to start Brindisa Tapas Kitchens with Monika and her business partner. Monika seems proud to have played a part in both his career and that of Chuse Valero at Bar Tozino, whom she recruited as her first ham carver after meeting him at a Barcelona trade fair.

Today, motorways and the AVE high-speed train whizz you from one Spanish city to another. But things were very different in the early days of Brindisa, Monika recalled. "If you wanted to transport something from the west of Spain to Barcelona, it cost the same as transporting it from Barcelona to London. And buying produce from Mallorca,

Menorca, or especially the Canary Islands was incredibly expensive."

A lot of Brindisa's products come from north Spain, because that's where the land is more fertile, she explained. "Many British people, when they go to Spain, go to the south because of the sun. But there's too much sun for a lot of agriculture."

She realised that if she was to make Brindisa a success, she needed to be based in London. To begin with, she rented some space in a Bermondsey warehouse before eventually taking out a lease on a warehouse in Winchester Square, close to Borough Market, and in 1995 she began selling from it at what she called open evenings. "I just decided to invite friends and family to our warehouse, so they could buy things, because we were still struggling to get retailers to stock all our products."

To her surprise, the open evenings turned out to be a great success. "That was really the moment that I thought, we have to reach the public ourselves, in a way that we can't do via the trade."

In the mid-1990s, Borough Market wasn't the kind of shrine for foodies it is today. It was still a wholesale fruit and vegetable market. I can remember walking past it late at night and seeing long lines of trucks and vans parked up in the surrounding streets. In 1997, Monika persuaded the trustees of the market to allow her to rent a stall in it. Neal's Yard soon followed and then other food businesses. "We were here in Borough when it was a ghost town. It was quite easy to get lorries in back then. You can't do that now", she said.

This was when you could still wander among the market's stalls without feeling that you were caught up in a crowd going to a football match. The open-top tourist buses never came south across the river, still thinking there was nothing worth seeing there. It was only those who lived or worked in offices nearby who knew about Borough Market.

I mentioned to Monika that I might have played a small part in increasing Borough Market's popularity. Back in the late 1990s when I was struggling to make it as a freelance journalist, I pitched an idea to the editor of *Just the Job*, the *Evening Standard*'s Monday supplement, for an article about the people selling food at the market. He liked it, booked a photographer, and I went along and interviewed half a dozen stall holders, including a woman who sold dozens of varieties of chillies and a farmer who made Cheshire cheese. It seemed that, after the article was published, numbers to the market started to increase.

Monika's next step was to open a shop in the market. She saw this as a way of getting Spanish food better known to the public while at the same time showing to Spanish restaurants the kind of products Brindisa was importing. The market's growing popularity as a destination for foodies led Monika in 2004 to open a tapas restaurant on the edge of it.

Borough Market's success has put it on the tourist map, something that hasn't been entirely beneficial, she said. "We still have shoppers, but there are lots of people who just come to take photos and buy a snack. Borough Market's problem is that it's become too popular with tourists. It's no longer the authentic shoppers' paradise it was at the beginning. The problem is that, when anywhere becomes popular, the temptation for the traders is just to offer fast food. It then becomes a hang-out and shopping takes second place. The trustees are trying to bring the market back to its roots when it was all about ingredients and quality producers."

While you can buy excellent food at Borough Market, I get the impression that some stallholders offering takeaways are more concerned with what they cash up at the end of a day than the quality of what they serve. Nevertheless, Borough Market has been terrific in changing the food landscape of London and providing opportunities to buy fresh and previously unavailable ingredients. It has also been the catalyst for other markets and farmers' markets that have sprung up across the capital.

As well as in Borough Market, Brindisa now operates restaurants in South Kensington, Soho, Piccadilly, and Shoreditch. Its menus are rooted in traditional ingredients, Monika explained, with plenty of vegetables on offer, something that wasn't always the case with Spanish food. "We don't want whacky stuff going on, but we want to be contemporary. We're not trying to be a Michelin-star restaurant. We want our ingredients to speak for themselves. I'm never going to compromise on them."

But by far the most interesting development with Brindisa was the opening of a restaurant in Barcelona. How big a decision was this? "We weren't really looking to open a restaurant there. But an opportunity was presented to us and it felt completely right. Obviously, we have a strong link with Barcelona, because that's where I lived before starting Brindisa, and its where my brother lives, and he's a key adviser.

For a British company to open a restaurant in a Spanish city is unheard of. But a British restaurant serving up not just Spanish but Catalan dishes must have raised a few eyebrows. So how much of a gamble was it? "It was risky. But we are not there to teach the Catalans how to cook. Half the team are Catalan anyway. There are so many Catalan chefs who come to London to cook. So why can't they go back home and cook and we can have an exchange between the two cities? And our non-Spanish chefs at Brindisa are given an opportunity to do a stint at the Barcelona restaurant to learn Catalan cooking techniques and the tapas culture."

So competitive is the London restaurant scene that many of those going into it seem to think that they must have some new or crazy idea to win customers. As I write this, a restaurant serving insects has recently opened. Monika doesn't believe in following the latest food trend, or that she must keep coming up with new ideas. "You have to hold your nerve. If the food is irresistible, you don't have to keep changing it. A lot of restaurants have a single theme. You can have a meatball restaurant, and there's a new one that just serves birds. I think this is brilliant, but I don't think we have to do this to stay popular. One of the most important things for Brindisa is to keep up to date with developments in food in Spain."

Is she looking more at what's going on in Spain rather than what's going on in London, then? "We have to try and do both. There's no point in cutting back on our excellent menus just to fit in with a fashion for, say, just doing rice. An only-rice restaurant in London would struggle. There are not many themes in Spanish cooking that would sustain a whole restaurant."

How, then, does she see Brindisa developing? "We're very happy with what we are doing. Our warehouse in Balham, what I call the mothership, is absolutely crucial, so developing our technologies there in terms of efficiency is really important."

Because Brindisa supplies Sainsbury's, Waitrose, and Ocado, I was surprised when she said that supermarkets were not part of her initial business strategy. "We choose quite carefully who we deal with because some of the companies we work with in Spain don't have the capacity to provide large amounts. Our aim now is to balance relationships with independent traders and the supermarkets, so the quality of the produce we sell is not compromised. You have to keep your USP."

Given Brindisa's reputation, unsurprisingly, there's no shortage of companies in Spain wanting to sell their products to it. "Quite a lot of Spanish producers approach the British market a little bit over-confident ... British supermarkets are very dominant and they also have a lot of own-label products: Tesco Finest, and so on. This slightly undermines the supplier label, which is not necessarily what the British look for."

How do you mean? I asked.

"Well, the majority of people want something that is easy, that they can understand, and that looks nice. And hopefully the contents will deliver. People shop with their eyes in England more than they do in Spain. If you have a badly packaged product from Spain, no matter how good it is inside, there's no chance in England, while in Spain it might sell really well. And what you might put into the branch of a supermarket in London might be different to what you would put into one in the countryside."

She doesn't rule out opening more restaurants, but has no intention of any kind of rapid expansion of the Brindisa brand, as this would end up diluting it. "If you want to keep it a personal business, which is what Brindisa thrives on being, I don't think we can grow that much more without losing a lot."

Would she think of one day taking the Brindisa brand to big cities such as Birmingham or Liverpool? "Not at the moment. It's not part of our current thinking. The problem with growing in that way is it's a matter of choosing not so much what you want to do but what problems you want to encounter. So if we start opening up in Manchester or in Scotland, then we have a whole new set of problems we aren't used to coping with. We'd much rather consolidate closer to home and, if we were to go anywhere, we would go back to source. If the source is Spain, then let's get closer to Spain."

The growing popularity of tapas is not entirely beneficial to Spanish cuisine, Monika maintains. "The upside is that Spanish tapas breaks down all the formalities of eating one dish per person. There's nothing worse than going to a conventional restaurant where you both order a dish and you would rather have your partner's than the one you've got. The idea of a tapas experience is that you never have that situation because you are going to share everything. The downside is that tapas is all people really want from Spain. They don't want the formal dining, because they get this from French or Italian and they have a much better track record."

What are some of the major challenges in establishing a successful restaurant? "It has to be the quality of the food and how you treat your team. The team needs to be well informed, well trained, and well recompensed for their efforts. Having a good chef and a good kitchen team is fundamental."

Despite having created such a successful business, one that now employs over 250 staff, she doesn't think that she has a great business mind. "What I do is see the opportunities. With our restaurants, I brought in an experienced operations director from the industry to come and join me and then he became a partner. He knows how these businesses run." I suspected she was being modest about her skills. When I had suggested that a recently closed fish and chip shop along Lordship Lane in East Dulwich would make an excellent tapas bar, she had immediately shaken her head and said that, while lots of people went there to eat at weekends, there wasn't enough footfall during the week.

While Monika comes across as someone who is quite calm, I suggested that the stress of keeping Brindisa running smoothly, dealing with suppliers, sorting out staff issues, and recruiting the right calibre chefs must keep her awake some nights.

"I don't run Brindisa on my own. I have an extensive group of incredible people who run the business on the ground", she said.

To recharge her batteries, she enjoys hill walking in England and Spain, and yoga. She's been on several yoga retreats, including one in Sri Lanka.

One secret of Brindisa's success, she believes, is a combination of its heritage, its brand, what it sells, and the ethics that underpin it. "We were the first people to bring over Spanish hams and *chorizo* to Britain, and were the first on many levels. And this is inspiring for the people who work in the restaurant, because we have such a history. We pioneered Spanish food in Britain in a way nobody else did in the Eighties and Nineties. The other is the quality of the food. I've always insisted on the best even if we've now got a middle quality in some ranges."

Looking back, does she think she has made any major mistakes in the way she has done things?

"Mistakes?"

"Things that you might have done differently in hindsight?"

"Well, yes, there were mistakes", she said after a long pause. "But some are too sensitive to mention. Growing a business means dealing with a lot of people and making decisions with your head rather than your heart, and that's really hard for me. You have to realise that as you grow you can't make everybody happy all the time."

If she had known more about how to manage people, she might have done some things differently, she said. "I just think it's very difficult to do anything perfectly in life, let alone in business. I made the best decision at the time with the knowledge that I had, or the choices that I had."

Monika has written a book about Brindisa, *Brindisa: The True Food of Spain*, which is due out later in the year. For it, she travelled around Spain meeting friends and suppliers, and obtaining recipes and information about ingredients and how food is produced. She stayed at an olive oil mill in Andalusia, spent time with a fantastic home cook in Alicante, and went back to visit the restaurant she worked at in her teens on the Costa Brava.

"It was suggested to me a long time ago that I write a book, but I felt then that I couldn't do it justice, because of the business and running a family", she said. "I worked with Sheila Keating, a ghost writer, who knew how to structure a book like this. It's really a book about home cooking."

You can't buy that sheep's milk cheese in a tin from Brindisa's shop in Brixton, as the manufacturer stopped making it some time ago. However, it might soon be on sale again, as his son has bought some sheep and is planning to restart production. The shop sells a wide range of Spanish cheese, including Garrotxa, a pure white cheese with a grey milk rind, from Catalonia; La Peral, creamy and speckled with blue, from Asturias; and La Retorta, slightly runny and from Extremadura.

After the interview, as Monika walked me to the door, she looked through the window at the passers-by outside on Atlantic Road and said, reflectively, "I'm terribly proud of Brindisa, but you can't be complacent. Keeping a business interesting is just as challenging as setting it up. I don't stop thinking about Brindisa."

8. Barcelona! Barcelona!

"For the first time in London we started to see serious investments in Spanish restaurants ... and companies being created."

María José Sevilla, Spanish Trade Commission

As a child I had eaten *paella* that came out of a packet and, not knowing any better, I thought it was delicious. But it wasn't until the early 1990s when I was working for a charity, based in an ugly Sixties building off Edgware Road, that I first tasted authentic Spanish food. My first taste of Spanish food came in the early 1990s when I worked for a charity based in an ugly Sixties building off Edgware Road. At lunchtimes, I would sometimes go to the Spanish deli at the bottom of the street, where I usually ordered the same thing: a slice of *tortilla* in a floury bap. The matronly woman who served me would always give me a slightly puzzled look each time I asked her to smother it with mayonnaise and sprinkle black pepper on it. "No, a little more mayonnaise, please," I would say. I got the impression that this wasn't how you were supposed to eat *tortilla* in Spain. Her husband, who always seemed to be operating the machine that sliced ham, would sneak a disapproving glance at me, probably thinking, "Here's that mayonnaise man again." His wife would swiftly cut open the bap and place the tortilla inside it, before slicing it in two, sliding it onto a paper plate, and wrapping it in a brown paper bag. I'd return to the office with my booty and devour it at my desk, savouring every bite and usually managing to dribble mayonnaise down my shirt. I don't think I've ever eaten a better sandwich. It was so good I can still taste it even after all these years.

Next to the deli was a small Spanish restaurant, Don Pepe. With its faded striped awning, it looked like it had been there for years. However, I never visited it. Those were the days when a night out for me meant going to the pub, not to a restaurant. Discovering that Don Pepe was still in business, I emailed the owner, Pepe Garcia, mentioning the *tortilla* I used to buy from the deli, and he invited me to meet him one afternoon for some tapas and a glass of wine. I was delighted at the prospect of finding out how the restaurant began and how it had changed over the years.

Pepe, dressed in a tweed jacket and shirt and tie, was standing at the bar when I arrived. A jovial man in his Sixties, with thick eyebrows, he greeted me warmly and immediately asked his long-serving head waiter, Luis, to bring a plate of *tortilla*.

"To drink?" he asked, gesturing to the bottles behind the bar.

"A Galician red," I said, remembering that Pepe had told me on the phone that he came from Galicia. I thought I might impress him.

"We don't have red wine from Galicia," he replied, shaking his head. "Not so good. Galicia produces good white wine, the *albariño*. Our red wine is Rioja."

"Well, Rioja's always a winner," I said.

"You know, it was me who provided the *tortilla* to the deli," he beamed.

"Was it?"

"Yes, it was me! Was it good?"

"It was delicious!"

"You liked it?"

"I loved it."

He purred with pleasure and then explained that, after a change of owner, the deli had closed a few years back. He didn't say what had happened to the couple who used to run it.

After another glass of wine, Pepe ushered me downstairs to an empty restaurant. The room had a rustic appearance, with mock Tudor beams and white walls decorated with paintings of rural scenes, including one of a man playing the bagpipes, and another of King Juan Carlos in an army uniform. I suspected that the decor hadn't changed in years.

"We need to get a picture of the new king," said Pepe thoughtfully, looking around. "You know," he said, "I always thought bagpipes came from Scotland."

"So did I."

"They come from Galicia."

"Do they?"

"Yes, yes. From Galicia."

I'd heard that Galicia, a green and often wet region of north-west Spain, seems to have more in common with the Celtic world than it does with the Mediterranean. It also seems to rain more there than it does in Ireland, which is saying something.

Although Pepe is proud of his Galician roots, he emphasised that the restaurant is definitely Spanish, not Galician. "The Barcelona fan club used to meet here, you know," he said, topping up my glass.

Pepe likes to talk, but his strong accent and tendency to hop from one subject to another left me struggling at times to understand him. Even so, I grasped that he grew up on his father's farm in Lugo, and went to catering college after leaving school. Following a spell in a hotel, he came to Britain when he was twenty, going to work for six months in a hotel in Conwy, north Wales.

In the 1960s, Spaniards could only come to London if they had a work permit, and these were generally restricted to jobs in the low-skilled service industries. Women were usually employed as domestic servants, cleaners, or chambermaids in hotels, while men worked as cooks and porters in hospitals or, occasionally, as chefs in restaurants. Pepe was keen to point out that, unlike many Galicians, he didn't come to the UK to escape economic problems back home. For him, it was more of an adventure.

When the job in Wales ended, Pepe came to London for a week, intending to return home to Galicia, but instead became head waiter at St Ermin's Hotel, near St James's Park Tube station, where he stayed for over two years.

At the time, there were very few Spanish restaurants or bars in London. Those that did exist had been opened primarily for immigrant Spaniards, some of whom had come as refugees during the three-year long Spanish Civil War, which erupted in 1936. Many of them settled in North Kensington, Notting Hill, or Pimlico.

The R Garcia & Sons supermarket (no relation to Pepe Garcia) on Portobello Road opened in 1957, making it the oldest Spanish shop in Britain. When I lived in Kensal Green, I would often take the short walk to Portobello Road on Saturday mornings. I loved going there because of the fantastic atmosphere of the market and because, with its houses washed in yellows, pinks, and blues, it had a Mediterranean feel about it. I'd sometimes look in the window of Garcia's, intrigued by the *chorizo*, bottles of olive oil, and tins of squid in black ink. It all looked so exotic and appealing. But, knowing little about Spanish food, I never had the courage to actually go inside.

Pepe has fond memories of his early days in London and the Spanish places he'd sometimes go to for a night out. He talked nostalgically about The Costa Brava on Charing Cross Road, and Martina's off Regent Street. He was involved for a number of years with Centro Galego de Londres, which began in a pub in Notting Hill Gate before relocating to Harrow Road. When I asked him if he still went there, he pulled a face and said he didn't like the way it was run nowadays.

Keen to make his mark in London, he left his job at St Ermin's Hotel, teamed up with two business partners, and, in 1971, opened a Spanish club on Edgware Road. "It was very busy from the day we opened. We had dinner and dancing. All the customers were Spanish."

The success of the club led Pepe and his business partners to decide to open a restaurant in Frampton Street serving tapas. For some reason or other, the business relationship ended and, in 1974, Pepe and his brother Alejandro took over the restaurant, eventually converting the storage room downstairs into a seating area.

So did many English people come in those early days? "Yes, yes, English people came to the restaurant. The Spanish would come at weekends, but the English would come in the week. We were very expensive when we first opened. But we were providing the kind of Spanish food no one else was providing, and using fresh ingredients."

Most of the seafood used in the restaurant was flown in by plane from Galicia, and Pepe would drive to Heathrow Airport to collect it. The novelty of a tapas bar in London didn't go unnoticed in the media: he was featured on BBC TV and was the subject of a TV programme back in Spain.

Luis, who has worked at Don Pepe for thirty-two years, and who seemed to regard Pepe almost as a brother, arrived with another bottle of Rioja and then brought several tapas dishes: prawns in garlic and olive oil, Jamón Serrano, *calamari*, *padrón* peppers, *chorizo* in wine, and grilled octopus.

A few minutes later, Luis returned with a large leather-bound book of black and white photographs published to celebrate Galicians in the diaspora, and placed it on the table. "This is Pepe," he announced, turning to a page with a photo of a smartly dressed man sitting in the back of a limousine, looking very much like a mafia boss. The photo was taken in 1989. Another photo, taken in the same year, showed

Pepe with his brother, wife, and a dozen staff, including three chefs, at the restaurant, standing behind a display of seafood, fish, and bottles of wine. These were the days when, surprisingly, the restaurant was popular with Japanese tourists.

I got the impression that, back then, Pepe was quite ambitious, although he downplayed this. How else can you explain that, in the 1990s, he ran three other Spanish restaurants in London: in Bayswater, Bell Lane in the City, and Clerkenwell? Later on, he bought a seventeen-bedroom hotel near Hampton Court Palace, where he put on flamenco dancing each month. He sold it in 2013, but didn't say why.

"I could have been much better off," he said wistfully.

"Do you think so?" I said, surprised at this remark.

"Yes. Sometimes I've been too soft in business."

I found the images of Pepe I'd seen in the photos hard to square with how he thought of himself. In them, he looked prosperous, confident, and like a man with a purpose.

Nowadays he doesn't spend that much time at Don Pepe, although, the previous week, he had cooked in the kitchen because the chef was on holiday. One of his daughters is also involved in running the restaurant, although she combines this with a senior position in a hotel.

"The area has changed a lot," he sighed. "It's now mainly Arab. There used to be five pubs near the restaurant."

For many years, the part of Edgware Road south of the Marylebone Flyover has been a kind of Beirut-on-Thames, with Lebanese and Syrian restaurants, shisha cafés, travel agents, and shops selling ostentatious furniture. But in recent years, the Arab community has spread north of the flyover to the streets around Don Pepe. I suspect that, given that most Arabs are Muslim and don't eat pork, a Spanish restaurant might seem unappealing.

Pepe has no plans to retire. As recently as 2014, he opened a tapas bar in Worthing. One of the reasons he chose the quiet Sussex coastal town, he said, was because it reminded him a little of Galicia.

Like everyone else I spoke to, he believes tapas is going to become even more popular in London. On the other hand, he didn't seem that impressed by some of the new Spanish restaurants that have opened. He struck me as someone very traditional, and I wondered if he thought the dishes some of them served were not traditional enough.

It's remarkable that he has kept Don Pepe going for over forty years. That's quite an achievement. Restaurants come and go, and Spanish restaurants are no exception. While writing this book, I stumbled across the names of numerous Spanish restaurants that had, for one reason or another, closed their doors. These include Castilla in Battersea Rise, Blanco's in Earls Court Road, Baradero in Poplar, and Fuego in the City. No doubt some just couldn't make enough money. With others, perhaps the owners decided to return to Spain. This was the case with César, who ran El Molino in Beckenham for twenty-five years. Following the death of his wife, he found himself coming home at the end of a long day in the restaurant to an empty house. "There's nothing here for me now. I want to go back to Galicia," he told me when I met him one evening. As César's son wasn't interested in taking over the restaurant, it could have become another casualty, but it was bought by a local man. Although he had no experience in providing Spanish food, he was determined to build on the loyal customer base César had established.

I wanted to learn more about how Spanish food had developed in London since those days when Pepe opened his restaurant. And few people have a better understanding about the rise of Spanish cuisine in London than María José Sevilla, the head of the food and wines department of the Spanish Trade Commission, the Spanish Embassy's commercial wing in London. She's also written a book about Basque cooking and presented a BBC TV series about the food of Spain. As well as this, she is an occasional chef instructor at the Culinary Institute of America in New York.

I met her at her smart office in the City. Immaculately dressed in a business suit, and with perfectly manicured nails, she comes across as someone who would expect the waiter to immediately take her coat when she entered a restaurant. She suggested that a pivotal moment in the rise of Spanish cuisine in London occurred in 1992 when the Olympics were staged in Barcelona, and Freddie Mercury and the opera singer, Montserrat Caballé, stood on the stage and belted out, "Barcelona! Barcelona!" to the world's TV cameras. "There was an explosion of interest in Spain then," she declared.

Prior to that, in the late 1970s, she continued, there had been a lot of excitement at the way chefs in the Basque country were updating Spanish food. "For many historical reasons, it had been left behind. The Basque country was the natural place for this to begin as it's where most people eat better and talk more about food. It is also a place where many French chefs, after the French Revolution, moved. And it's where the Spanish royal family had traditionally spent their holidays."

In *Au Revoir to All That: The Rise and Fall of French Cuisine*, Michael Steinberger points out that Spain was just beginning its transition to democratic rule after four decades of stifling right-wing dictatorship under Franco. "Franco's death in 1975 opened the doors to political, economic, and cultural renewal, and this sense of liberation and opportunity reached into the kitchens of Spain."

Hosting the World Cup in 1982 also helped Spain's rehabilitation in Europe. In the following decade, a number of Spanish restaurants opened across London, including La Rueda in Clapham, Bar Gansa in Camden, Meson Don Felipe in Waterloo, and Don Fernando in Richmond. What's interesting about this wave of Spanish restaurants is that hardly any of them were situated in the West End, the area of London that has witnessed the largest increase in Spanish restaurants in the last fifteen years or so. You can now choose from around forty in the area. Soho alone boasts fourteen. Most of those earlier ones appear to have been set up as neighbourhood restaurants rather than places that might attract a younger, more adventurous crowd. Beyond London, the chain, La Tasca, opened its first restaurant in 1993, in Manchester.

Many of the chefs weren't even Spanish. Spaniards working in the hospitality industry in London still tended to be waiters – like Manuel in *Fawlty Towers*. In *A Late Dinner*, Paul Richardson remarks, "In the late 1980s in London, the very idea of a Spanish chef sounded, at the very least, unusual, if not actually oxymoronic. In the wake of the nouvelle cuisine, creativity in restaurant cooking was still essentially the domain of the French, while the rustic cooking most valued at the time was undoubtedly Italian, and the gastronomic avant garde was most active in California. Spain simply didn't figure."

When I suggested to María that her TV series, *Spain on a Plate*, must also have helped to raise the profile of Spanish cuisine, she nodded. "Keith Floyd had made some programmes about food in Spain, but the controller felt it needed a more serious approach. So they commissioned me to do *Spain on a Plate*. When we were filming in Madrid, I spoke to a young chef who was creating a new concept of tapas. He was approaching the subject in a completely different way. From that moment I can see that, little by little, the whole thing started moving along."

In her book of the same name, she provides a wonderful snapshot of the different cooking styles in Spain. "The various cooking styles smell of fish and seafood fresh from the sea, of seasoned roast meat, and of the rich wines that are used in country chicken and partridge hotpots.

There are Mediterranean styles: olive green in colour, and tasting of olive oil and almonds, rice and saffron. There are other styles that reflect the interior with its mountains and shepherds, cheeses and honey, and pinto beans cooked in deep painted metal and enamel *pucheros*. Different again is the cookery of the villages that are snowbound in the winter, with flavours of rich stock and pork fat; of villages that slumber on in the silence of Castilla, the so-called lands of bread and wine; and those that bustle in vivacious Andalusia."

With the arrival of Ferran Adrià on the scene, Spanish cuisine, once thought of as inferior to French and Italian, had not just the gastronomic world talking about it but also people with serious money, claimed María. To capitalise on the fame of Adrià, the Spanish Trade Commission made a series of videos about investment. "The first one was about investing in Spanish gastronomy in the UK market. I realised how important Spanish food was becoming. The videos showed that you could make money in a place like London. And for the first time in London we started to see serious investments in Spanish restaurants … and companies being created."

Spanish food took off in London because of tapas and what chefs were doing in Spain, she insisted, pointing out that Iberica brought in a Michelin-star chef to design its menus. "And Brindisa was absolutely instrumental in the tapas world in London. Monika Linton not only brought Spanish food to the British, she also started importing Spanish products. She had a wonderful vision of the market."

The Spanish Trade Commission is putting a lot of energy into promoting Spanish cuisine. Its impressive web site, called "Foods and Wines from Spain", comes complete with interactive maps showing the food and wine from the different regions, interviews, recipes, and potted histories of various aspects of Spanish gastronomy. In 2015, María launched an initiative called "Eat Spain, Drink Spain" and visited wine fairs in London, Manchester, Cardiff, Edinburgh, and Winchester.

"Spanish restaurants are now opening in the regions and cities," she said. "How successful they will be, I don't know. Some towns in the north are quite depressed. Spanish restaurants are not cheap to run because you have to have very good ingredients. You can't make tapas like they used to do in England forty years ago."

"You can't?" I said.

"It was rubbish food! They weren't run by professionals."

This seemed a bit unfair, and I'm sure Pepe would disagree. Yet it's a common view among many of those involved in the more recent development of Spanish cuisine in London.

While María believes that some of the new Spanish restaurants are as good as you would find in Spain, she also thinks the portions served are sometimes too small and that there's a risk some diners might conclude they are being taken for a ride.

She has a point here. As much as I love Spanish food, I do have a gripe. A major difference between a restaurant in Spain and a Spanish restaurant in London is the menu. In Spain, the menu will often list three portion sizes: tapas, *media ración*, and *ración*, so you can choose whether you want a few bites of *calamari* or a more substantial amount. And obviously, the price reflects the size of the portion. However, in London, you are likely to pay five or six pounds for a small tapas plate. I remember how small the portions were at the Streets of Spain festival. At one Spanish restaurant in central London I visited with a friend, we paid nine pounds fifty for six tiny pieces of squid with a dollop of *alioli*. If we had each ordered the dish it would have come to nineteen pounds. This is very steep. When Bea and I came to pay the bill at another Spanish restaurant, in south-east London, we asked the waitress why we were being charged one pound seventy-five, not one pound, for each *croqueta de jamón* we had ordered for our son. The waitress pointed to the menu and, looking at it again, I saw that the price had been written as £1 ¾. I don't know if this was a deliberate attempt to deceive the customer, but it felt like it. And anyway, seven pounds for four bite-sized *croquetas de jamón* is pricey. It was no wonder that the restaurant was virtually empty. If María had a similar experience, I imagine she would click her fingers and summon the manager to her table.

At the moment in the UK, fine dining is a problem, she revealed, which is why tapas has been so successful. "Fine dining restaurants don't make a lot of money. Restaurants like a tapas bar can be very successful with the minimum of effort. You only need a good chef, a couple of waiters or whatever and off you go. If you are very good, everybody talks about you."

It goes without saying that the food in a restaurant is only as good as the chef. María maintains that, in the past, Spanish chefs didn't want to travel, preferring to remain in their home town with their friends and families. If the Spanish scene in London is to continue to grow, then Spanish chefs need to come, and they need to speak English. And if they do, they can make good money. When I saw a job vacancy from a leading tapas bar in the West End, I was astonished that the salary being offered was between £65, 000 and £75,000. I don't know why, but I had never imagined that chefs could earn that sort of money.

"If some of the Spanish chefs decide to head to the UK, then the scene will change," María predicted. "But at the moment they are not doing that. There's no space for fine dining. So any development has to be through tapas."

I think María is right. Tapas is casual dining, which is the major trend in the restaurant industry. And sharing small plates is a wonderful way to eat. You get to try different dishes rather than just have one and you can graze instead of having a full meal. As Anthony Rose and Isabel Cuevas observe in the introduction to *The Tapas Bar Guide*, published in 2014, "Thanks to new cooking techniques and a focus on products of the land, the recent transformation of Spanish gastronomy has turned the tapas concept into the most important phenomenon in Spanish culinary history."

9. The Sherry Man

"This is the only place outside of Spain that does sherry the right way, from barrels."

Tim Luther, Drake's Tabanco

I was looking for Drake's Tabanco, one of the Spanish bars and restaurants clustering around Charlotte Street, in a corner of the West End whose pavements are free of the usual crowds of tourists. Its owner had agreed to meet me to talk about sherry. However, when I still hadn't spotted it after strolling up and down Windmill Street a couple of times, I began to wonder if I might have the wrong address.

Eventually, I found the door and went inside. Tim Luther, the owner, was at a table, tapping away at his iPad, and didn't seem surprised that I had walked past the restaurant twice without noticing it. "Other people have had the same problem. I suppose we're not that prominent."

Tim admitted that, when Drake's opened its doors in 2013, it was a nerve-wracking time. On opening day, the builders left at six and customers started arriving through the doors at seven. Business got off to a flying start, though, when an *Evening Standard* wine writer turned up and wrote enthusiastically about the sherry on offer.

Drake's is based on the typical *tabanco* (a kind of tavern) found in Jerez de la Frontera, which is regarded as the sherry capital of Spain. The word "sherry" is the Anglicised form of Jerez. Drake's recalls Francis Drake's destruction of the Spanish navy near the port of Cádiz on Spain's Atlantic coast, when he took as his spoils 2,900 barrels of sherry. These he presented to the British court who, presumably, had a right old time getting through them.

With its dark wood interior, Drake's has a rustic feel. At the front is a bar, with barrels behind it, while down some steps is a restaurant at the back, with a *jamón* and *chorizo* bar circled by stools.

If Omar Allibhoy's mission in life is to introduce more people to tapas, then Tim's is to persuade them of the delights of sherry. He's another Englishman who has been seduced by the food and wine of Spain. Clean cut, with shortish brown hair, and dressed in jeans and a V-neck sweater, he could have passed for just another trendy media type rather than the bar's owner. Despite having worked in advertising, he's not that keen on doing publicity, which might explain his hesitating manner when answering my questions. He strikes me as the kind of person who would stand patiently while stuck in a long queue at the post office, even when everyone else had begun to voice their frustration.

"We wanted to bring a flavour of the *bodega*, the winery that produces the wine", he explained. "This is the only place outside of Spain that does sherry the right way, from barrels. We describe Drake's Tabanco as a tapas restaurant and a sherry bar. This is so we don't exclude people. If you just say you are a sherry bar, then suddenly you are narrowing your market. You would have a lot of people potentially not interested in you."

Customers who order a drink at Drake's are given free tapas, partly to recreate the Andalusian tradition and partly, of course, to encourage them to take a look at the menu, which boasts smoked scallop with garlic purée and beetroot, truffled goats cheese with honey, and "Tom Jones" fillet steak served with confit potatoes and East India gravy. Tim wants the menu to excite customers. "You look at the menu, you find something interesting, you look at it on the plate, you eat it and go, 'Wow!'. That's how it should be."

By comparison, if you go into a bar in Jerez, you are likely to end up disappointed, he maintains. "Some have a very poor food offering, because the love's not there. Since the economic crisis Jerez is a crumbling city. It's beautiful, but they can only afford what they can afford, which is often not the best sherry and not the best food."

For many people, me included, sherry has always seemed a slightly puzzling drink – half way between a wine and a spirit – drunk at Christmas or funerals and favoured by elderly ladies as their tipple. The sherry that most people drank when I was growing up was Harvey's Bristol Cream or VP. Until I met Tim, I was unaware that sherry begins life as a wine, but has grape spirit added to make it stronger, something that originated in pre-refrigeration days to ensure it would keep. After this, it is aged in large oak barrels and goes through what's called the *solera* system, a traditional ageing process in which young and old wines are progressively mixed together. When the sherry arrives at Drake's Tabanco in sealed containers, it is transferred to 125-litre aged oak barrels, which are topped up as and when required. Tim never allows the level of sherry in the barrels to fall below fifty litres.

"We're effectively creating our own mini *solera*", he said. "The base level we have in the barrels has been there since we opened and this adds complexity to the wine. For sherry lovers this is quite exciting. Our wines are as you would taste them in the winery. If you taste sherry out of a barrel, and then taste bottled sherry, the difference is evident."

The staff serve the sherry by lowering a *venenciador*, which resembles a spoon with a long handle, into a hole in the barrel and ladling it into a glass. Tim doesn't know of any other bars that serve it like this, even in Spain. "The only places that do this are sherry *bodegas*."

All his sherry comes from Fernando de Castilla in Jerez, who, he insists, is the best producer in Spain. "The sherry has been declassified in order to sell it to us in this format, because you are not allowed to bottle it outside of Jerez."

Because some companies were diluting sherry at one time to make bigger profits, he explained, the regulatory council that oversees the quality of sherry insists that it must be bottled before it leaves the *bodega*. Bizzarely, this means that Tim isn't allowed to use the word sherry, because what he sells is shipped from Jerez in vacuum-sealed plastic containers. "It is sherry. But we call it *fino* or *oloroso*. I understand where the DO (Denominación de Origen) is coming from, but it's a little bit ridiculous, because it is what it is."

Tim pointed out that while overall sales of sherry are going down, restaurant sales of the dry styles – *fino, manzanilla, amontillado, oloroso* – are going up. "This might be because Granny isn't here any more. And this is where the quality is. The stuff Granny drank, such as Crofts or Harvey's Bristol Cream, was artificially sweetened."

His solution to the image problem besetting sherry sounds quite radical. He thinks the name should be scrapped and replaced with, for example, *fino* or *amontillado*. "To my mind, these sherries are the best wines with food. They are phenomenal. If you throw crazy flavours and challenging ingredients at sherry it just seems to lap it up. There is a style of sherry that you can happily drink with a curry. There's styles of sherry that you can drink with artichokes, or even eggs, which are famously hard to pair with wine."

I wonder how this would go down with the sherry DO. I suspect such a move would be regarded as almost sacrilegious.

Tim runs three other Spanish restaurants, Copita in Soho, Copita del Mercado in Spitalfields, and Barrica, his first, situated around the corner from Drake's Tabanco. With their modern take on Spanish cuisine, they have garnered some glowing reviews from critics. Marina O'Loughlin raved that Copita was as good as the best tapas bar in San

Sebastián, while *Time Out* described it as "an authentic taste of modern Spain in the heart of Soho — and a sherry-lover's paradise." Barrica and Copita were awarded a Bib Gourmand in the 2014 edition of the *Michelin Guide*.

However, you can't please everyone, and a grumpy Jay Rayner in the *Guardian* complained that Drake's sherry list was too narrow, saying that he didn't think much of its attempt to recreate a rustic Jerez bar.

One of the main reasons why so many restaurants go out of business within the first year is that the owners failed to do their homework. Having a good idea is one thing, but you also have to find the right product, location, and market. When Tim decided to open a tapas bar in the West End, he identified the area around Charlotte Street, home to many media companies, as a good location. He knew from his time there working for an advertising agency that people in local offices like to go out a lot to eat and drink. He was right. When I worked as a TV researcher I sometimes went to the Channel 4 studios in Charlotte Street to record the studio segment, and we would often all go to a fantastic Italian restaurant nearby afterwards.

This is why Tim spent weeks wandering the streets and sitting in the corners of bars and restaurants, counting the number of customers. Eventually, he settled on vacant premises in Goodge Street, and in 2009 opened Barrica.

When he first thought of opening a Spanish bar, he considered Covent Garden and Soho, but felt that the former was too touristy and the latter too expensive. Intuitively, he felt that a Spanish restaurant around the northern end of Charlotte Street, which had few restaurants back then, would be a hit. "I wanted to find out which places were busy and which weren't, and discover why", he said. "You can find information on an area on the web, but there's no substitute for seeing it for yourself, going into the restaurants to see how busy they are, what they serve, what they charge, and what the footfall is."

Convinced that a Spanish bar would work, he persuaded his wife, Clare, to agree to remortgage their house in Earlsfield in south-west London, to raise capital. Starting a business is one thing; putting your house on the line is another. So how worried was she that it could all go wrong?

"She must have been a bit anxious but she certainly didn't show it", he said.

So she didn't think she could end up losing her home?

"I showed her my business plan, talked her through all my research of the area and of the product. She knows I am thorough. And she knew … that this really was what I wanted to do. It wasn't just a pipe dream."

Because of the huge gamble he was taking, Tim knew he had to be as certain as he could that he was choosing the right premises and location. Some restaurants fail for no other reason than being in the wrong place. "I felt I couldn't leave any stone unturned. I had one chance at opening a restaurant, and I needed to know for myself what the area was really like. I couldn't take other people's word. If the business didn't succeed in the way I wanted it to, then at least I could say I did my homework. I was there on a Saturday night over the course of two or three months. I was there on Monday lunchtime. When you are borrowing money and putting your house on the line, you can't go, 'Oh, well, the agent told me it was busy.'"

The premises in Goodge Street he identified for his tapas bar had been an Italian risotto bar. "I think what it was offering was a bit confused when I saw it. I don't know if they knew what they were, because they were trying to attract people in for salads and takeaways and they had a blackboard outside listing cocktails. It was all a bit fragmented."

Why did he think a tapas bar would work? Was it because Spanish food was becoming all the rage? "I didn't think Spanish food was catching on particularly, but I did think it was under-represented. And I still think it is, even with all the Spanish restaurants that have opened. It was more a case of the way of eating. This kind of high level, informal eating wasn't really around in 2009. Bar seats now are some of the most wanted seats in restaurants. People ask for them because they like to see things going on. You can talk to the staff behind the bar or, if there is a kitchen, you can watch the chefs."

It's not just tapas bars that offer the bar stool experience, he added. Russell Norman's Polpo restaurants, based on back street bars in Venice, have made this a key feature, as have some Indian, Japanese, and Greek restaurants.

Opening a restaurant is a nightmare, he conceded, adding that there were times when he wondered why he was doing it. "I know it's a cliché to say it's a passion and I'm not doing it for the money, but I think you have to have that to see you through all the bureaucracy and all those things that might otherwise stop you."

When Barrica opened, he had to do everything, from ordering the food and stocking the fridges to writing the specials on the blackboards and greeting customers at the door. He would arrive at 7.30 am and not get home until 1 am. "In the first two years I was doing a 100-hour week. I had Sundays off, which enabled me to be with my family, and also gave the feet a chance to stop throbbing for a bit. In the early days of the restaurant I was both wanting customers to come in but also hoping no one came in. I didn't have any experience and was worried that if people did come in they wouldn't enjoy it. I was terrified."

So when did he begin to realise that Barrica was going to be a success?

"A year after it opened, Barrica won Best Spanish Restaurant in the

Time Out eating and drinking awards. This gave us an instant uplift, which stayed with us for a whole year."

By the end of the second year he felt that he was financially secure and the bar had established itself. Tim is understandably upbeat about the future: Facebook and cosmetics brand Estée Lauder are moving into the area, Crossrail is due to start services from Tottenham Court Road station in 2018, and offices, shops, and flats are going up, such as on the site of the former Royal Mail sorting office in Rathbone Place.

Creating a true tapas experience in London isn't easy, he confessed. "A tapas bar is a bar serving really good food. It's upbeat, it's stools, it's ledges, there are no tables and you can't book. But you need high footfall for people to pop in, have tapas, and move on. And so opening a true tapas bar in the suburbs would be tricky because you wouldn't get that turnover. Perhaps a Spanish restaurant would work better out of town than a true tapas bar. But tapas bar culture in Spain is something everyone has grown up with. You have a couple of drinks and some tapas in one bar and move to another, and maybe go for a meal later. Here, people who have been to Spain know that, but, because you don't have a lot of tapas bars near each other, you go to one for lunch or for an evening."

Born in Germany to an Australian father and Scottish mother, Tim lived in Norway until he was five, before moving to a town in the Surrey commuter belt. Food has always been a huge part of his life because of his father, a chemical engineer. "He's not a chef or anything, but he's a very keen cook. He spent time in Paris and various cities, and at home we always had to score dishes and wines out of ten when we sat around the dinner table."

After leaving school, Tim went to university in Canterbury, but dropped out in the second term. "I chose film studies because it was a subject I liked, but I didn't really want to go to university." Various jobs followed, including delivering computers around the M25, helping a friend who ran a jewellery business, and humping scaffolding around building sites.

He then moved into advertising, where he became an account manager – one of his clients manufactured incontinence pads. He admitted that he was hopeless at it. Did his experience in advertising help him when he was planning to open Barrica? "I don't think so. Now you've asked that question I might go home and think, 'Oh, maybe it did.' But I don't think it did. What helped me was what's inside of me. That might sound a bit corny. It was determination but also a genuine love of food, drink, and people."

Eventually he quit advertising, deciding that he wanted to work in something he enjoyed, and landed a job at Albion Wines as a van driver, delivering to restaurants. Soon he started trying to sell it. "I would stop at restaurants on my route and say, 'Here's a list, and maybe you want to consider us when you buy wine.' It got to the stage when I wasn't out in the van very much."

It was when he began travelling with his boss to some of the vineyards in Spain that he became hooked on the food and the culture, and the seeds of his later ambition were sown. "We'd spend the day there and then, in the evenings, go on tapas crawls in the towns and cities. Like here, not every tapas bar in Spain is a good tapas bar, but when it's good it's fantastic. You get that whole upbeat social aspect to going out, where you're standing in a bar and it's very energetic. That whole environment of eating and drinking and having fun at the same time is a winner for me."

Seeing how wine was made, understanding its different grape varieties and styles, and learning the geography of the different areas, started to give him a knowledge of Spanish wine. He took some wine exams, but never went on to do the diploma, he confessed. "I've never been one for exams. They scare me and make me think I'm still at school doing A-levels."

There is no right or wrong when it comes to wine, he insisted. "So much of it is a matter of taste. There's nothing that beats experience and building up a knowledge through tasting, and understanding why a wine tastes the way it does. In our restaurants we always ask customers what kind of style of wine they like, because there's no point recommending a full-bodied red wine to someone when they like Pinot Noir. You need to understand what the customer wants to make a good recommendation."

Tim became a member of the Albion sales team and, as it was small, was involved in choosing any new wines brought into the portfolio. Discovering the world of wine was a turning point for him. This was when he first hatched the idea to open a Spanish restaurant.

But it was over three years before he saw his dream come true. So what was the process? Did he just decide one day that he wanted to run a restaurant, and then the idea grew and grew? "Absolutely. That's exactly how it was. I didn't have any experience. I think I pulled a pint in a pub when I was eighteen or something, but that was literally it. I was keen on having my own business and I spoke to a couple of friends who had pubs and a restaurant. They told me I would have to work hard. That didn't put me off. It all takes time. You have the idea, you find funding, find chefs, decide menus, those sort of things. And, of course, there is the simple thing of finding a premises. It's one thing to be able to afford somewhere in central London, another to find it, and another to get the deal to go through."

Finding the right staff and retaining them is one of the biggest challenges for any restaurateur. While there are plenty of chefs out there, when it comes to front of house staff, it's a different matter. Serving food in a restaurant isn't considered a vocation in Britain. In restaurants in Spain, and also in Italy and France, you can find immaculately dressed men in their fifties who have been waiting on tables for twenty or thirty years and are proud of it. They see their job as a profession. In contrast, being a waiter in Britain is seen as something students or migrants do, a job between jobs, or something to bring in a bit of extra cash. Tim doesn't hide his delight that several staff who joined Barrica when it first opened are still with him.

His advice to any would-be restaurateurs is not to do it if you have any doubts, no matter how excited you might be. And if you do go ahead, then you will need to be very patient and know when to say no. Opening the restaurant is a leap of faith, he suggested. "You have to do your homework but you also have to say, sod it, I'm going to go for it."

I liked his belief that there's a distinction between service and hospitality in a restaurant. We've all been to restaurants where, although the staff smile and say the right things, it feels more mechanical than genuine. "You can run a good service, but you have to be hospitable. You have to have characters in the building, on the floor, engaging with customers in the right way. And they have to be made to feel that, when they come in, they are going to have a good time in here. Sometimes people say to me, 'You're always talking about staff smiling.' If you walk down the street and someone smiles at you, it's almost impossible not to smile back. It's such a simple thing. It's all about giving the people who are paying your wages the best possible experience you can."

Tim enjoys cooking at home for his family and friends. He gave a wry smile when I mentioned an article I'd just read saying that the kitchen is the new shed, for men. "I enjoy following recipes," he said, "but because I'm around the chefs in the restaurants, I pick up tips and look at food in a different way." On a couple of occasions, when his restaurants have had staffing problems in the kitchen, he's had to don an apron. "I loved it because I had someone telling me what to do, rather than me telling someone what to do, which happens a lot in the course of my day. I said to the head chef, tell me what you want me to do and I'll do it. No one is going to care more than me about chopping that potato the right way."

If he had his time again, maybe he would have gone to catering college, he said, becoming reflective. "I don't know if I would have had the natural flair to be a great chef, but I would certainly have tried."

Spanish food in Britain is going through an exciting time, he believes. "It used to be that Spanish food was not considered as good as French or Italian in terms of quality. But Ferran Adrià from elBulli and all the chefs that have come out of there have been a tremendous influence on people's opinion of Spanish cuisine. The sherry, *jamón*, olive oil, and other raw ingredients from Spain, are up there with the best in the world."

Even so, he isn't planning to open another Spanish restaurant at the moment, but, surprisingly, has branched out into burgers, opening a burger bar in Cambridge with a business associate in 2015, with plans to open more around the country. "We provide craft beer on tap, so it's a proper bar. We do two or three "Ibérico" burgers, which go down very well. We did think of creating the first Ibérico burger bar, but then we thought: niche is OK, but it would be better to capture the wider market. We might be wrong, of course."

When I asked if the reason he opened the restaurant was, in a way, to bring joy to people, Tim gave a look of recognition. "Yes, it's not far removed from that at all. You saying that reminds me of when a master at school asked me what I wanted to do afterwards and I said – and I know it sounds cheesy – that I wanted to make people happy. And I guess this is actually fulfilling that answer. Through serving the food and drink I enjoy the most, and employing great people with smiles on their faces, and creating a good product and good value, I hope people leave happy. That's what it's all about."

10. Making a Name

"Spain is a country with seventeen countries in it. We are really regional and local."

José Pizarro, Pizarro

Flashing a smile and waving through the window at another passer-by, José Pizarro mouthed, "How are you?"

"I know everyone around here", he said with satisfaction, taking a sip of his espresso. "I know all my neighbours. You know, walking from here to José can take me half an hour.

"Half an hour?" I said.

"Yeah, absolutely. People stop me and I stop them."

I was sitting with him one morning in Pizarro, his restaurant in Bermondsey Street, once a rather shabby back street near London Bridge Station but now dotted with restaurants and home to both the Fashion and Textile Museum and the White Cube art gallery. Former warehouses have been turned into swanky flats or architects' offices. Further up the street is José, a tiny tapas bar on a corner, which José opened after leaving Brindisa's tapas bar by Borough Market, where he was head chef. Padstow is often nicknamed Padstein, because Rick Stein seems to have virtually taken over the Cornish fishing town with his clutch of businesses. I can't resist wondering if people will start calling Bermondsey Street Bermonzarro Street. If they do, José would "absolutely love it".

I'd eaten at Pizarro a couple of years before with Bea and some friends. The first thing I had noticed when we queued to be seated was the picture frames on the brick walls. They were empty. I tried to imagine why this was, but couldn't see what the point of it might be, other than to get you thinking along these same lines. Between us, we ordered cod fritters, meatballs, octopus with creamy potatoes, and a pork burger with fries. While I thought the food was good, the portions seemed quite small. The waiting staff were struggling to keep up with the stream of customers coming through the door. At one point, a waitress bringing a dish accidentally knocked over a bottle of water on our table, breaking the small plate containing olives and bread. She apologised, gathering up the plate and olives and bread, and went to get a replacement bottle of water. However, she didn't bring replacement olives and bread. The highlight of the meal for me was not the food but the small red *pimentón* tin the bill arrived in. I thought that was a nice touch. It now sits on a shelf in my office, but I didn't mention this to José.

José was dressed in a grey V-neck sweater, jeans, and trainers. For a man who always says he loves to eat a lot, he was very slim. He had just returned from the Taste of Abu Dhabi food festival, where, standing in a tent in forty-five degree heat, he had shown off his cooking skills. Earlier in the year he had attended a similar event in Dubai. "As you know, Spanish food at the moment is so fashionable, even in an Arab country, where they don't eat pork, which is one of the things in Spain we are good at producing."

So would he be tempted to establish a restaurant out there, like a host of celebrity chefs, including Jamie Oliver, Gary Rhodes, and Marco Pierre White, have done? He said, "my friend, I'm open to anything. At the moment, I'm very happy and London is home for me. I've lived here for nearly sixteen years. But you never know what will happen in the future."

If one man has helped to popularise Spanish food in London in the last few years, then you could argue it's José. In doing this, has done what, he maintains, for a long time Spaniards were not very good at doing. In 2014, the Spanish government bestowed on him a Marca España award, given to Spaniards overseas for promoting Spanish culture. In the same year, he was also named Extremaduran of the Year. José is certainly on a roll. When Food Network wanted someone to film a Spanish special for its series, *The Big Eat*, they chose José. He's received other awards, including *Harper's Magazine*'s On-trade Personality of the Year 2012 and *The Travel Magazine*'s 2012 Newcomer of the Year in food and wine. He was delighted to be asked to be a keynote speaker at the first Gastronomy Congress, held at the Hurlingham Club, where he appeared alongside Ferran Adrià, whom, predictably, he praises for putting Spanish food on the map.

To people in Britain, José is best known as the man with the cheeky chappie smile who crops up occasionally on BBC1's *Saturday Kitchen*. When the brilliant James Martin presented the show, José would often appear, fizzing with energy and saying, in his slightly camp way, "James, you are gonna love this! Believe me."

Although José has made a dozen appearances on the show, he didn't get off to a promising start. "The first time I was on it, I couldn't understand James and James couldn't understand me. My accent was very strong – it's still very strong – but his accent was also very strong. I didn't know what he was telling me. But from the first day we had a very good feeling between us. It's difficult because you have to think in a language that's not yours and you have to cook – and you have to be careful that you don't say fuck! If you say that, you are out of the BBC."

Guest chefs on the show, which is filmed at studios in Clapham, have only one rehearsal and their dish must be cooked in around eight minutes.

"Have you ever forgotten to put an ingredient in?" I asked.

"I think so", he grinned mischievously. "But I enjoy appearing on the show. It's fun. TV helps my business. I'm not someone who wants to be a TV chef. I've had a few proposals from TV companies to do things, but I didn't feel comfortable, so I told them no."

And, of course, he appeared in that Rick Stein TV series about Spain that first got me interested in Spanish cuisine. José hasn't yet joined the top tier of publically-recognisable chefs, but he's rising fast. He said he had an amazing time working with Stein and his team. They spent four or five days together. "Rick is a good friend now. He's a guy you love to spend time with because you learn so much. He's just a wonderful person. It's not because he knows a lot about food; it's because he knows a lot about life. And for me to be in Spain teaching something to a guy who knows everything was incredible."

José also appeared in a programme with Rick Stein about the food Spaniards eat at Christmas. "We had a proper Christmas – but I think it was in September", he said, adding that the roast shoulder of lamb he cooked was very popular with the viewers. "Many people told me afterwards that they had followed the recipe and liked it so much that they no longer bought turkey for their Christmas dinner."

I learned that he's writing his third cook book. His first two were entitled *Seasonal Spanish Food* and *Spanish Flavours*. This new one is about the food of the Basque country. He spent a week there travelling around with a photographer. Juan Mari Arzak has written the introduction, something that should help to boost sales. "It needs to sell well, because this could be the start of a series of books on the regions of Spain. It's very exciting, but there is lots to do."

So does he find it difficult to choose which recipes to include? "When you write a recipe you have to remember that it's not going to be a professional who will be cooking it." When he's thinking of including a recipe in a book, he will cook it several times and then give it to people to taste.

The week before, Bea and I had eaten at El Pirata, a charming tapas bar tucked away in Mayfair, and we had finished our meal by sharing a *crema Catalana*, which she maintained was the best she had tried anywhere. So I wondered what he thought of Spanish desserts. He shook his head. "You know, Spain is not big on desserts. When I'm writing a cookery book, desserts are always a struggle."

He's someone who understands the value media can bring to his business and he recognises that he has become a brand. He is the face of Tapas Fantasticas and also lent his name to endorse various Spanish products, including Estrella Damm beer and a brand of olive oil. If you have twenty-five pounds to spare after your meal at Pizarro, you can buy a signed book and José Pizarro bag.

José's journey to being an acclaimed Spanish chef in London began in the village of Talaván in Extremadura. He grew up on a farm, where his father grew vegetables and raised cows and hens. Yet it sounds like his parents struggled at times under the hardships of the Franco regime. Was it really true that he had once eaten fox?

"Absolutely. I've tried fox, I've tried dogs, I've tried cats. People didn't have money back then."

I just couldn't imagine ever eating animals like these. José's words reminded me of what Laurie Lee wrote in *As I Walked Out One Midsummer Morning*, his account of a journey through Spain in the 1930s as it slid into civil war: "I'd come through poor stone villages, full of wind and dust, where mobs of children convoyed me through the streets, and where priests and women quickly crossed themselves when they saw me, and there was nothing to buy except sunflower seeds."

José's mother was always busy in the kitchen, he remembers, and he has many recollections of food while growing up: the baby goat stew she used to cook with red peppers, garlic, and wine, and the partridge his grandmother would cook at Christmas, filling the kitchen with the smell of burning feathers. The reason he includes burgers on his menus is because his mother used to make them.

"I was always in touch with the food, but not with the cooking, because I wasn't allowed in the kitchen! My mum used to say, 'Go away from here!' so I had to help my dad instead."

He sensed early on that there was a bigger and far more interesting world to be discovered beyond the rural Spain he was so familiar with. "When I was a teenager, I couldn't see myself living in a small village looking after the cows. I saw my dad getting up at five every morning and doing that. But I never thought I was going to be a chef." When he was fourteen, he moved to the provincial capital Cáceres, a walled medieval city. He went off to Seville after leaving school, to study to be a dental technician. But after completing the course, and while he was waiting to hear about a job, he realised that he didn't want to spend the rest of his life making moulds for people's teeth. "I thought, I have to do something. I started to think about the ingredients and flavours of my mum's cooking, and decided to do a cookery course."

He enrolled at a catering college and, in his second year, got a job in a restaurant specialising in roasts. "I asked to work for free. This was the first time I had really cooked properly. After a while they offered me a job and said, 'Why don't you study and work at the same time?' But if you are a chef you can't do this. You don't have time. Many of the things I cooked in the restaurant – roasting lamb, suckling pig – were what I had seen my mum doing."

So what was his first experience in a professional kitchen like? He leaned forward, screwing up his face, and said, "My head chef was a bitch! Yeah. He pushed me a lot. A lot … But now I have to say thank you to him because he taught me all about working in a kitchen. You need to be clever and creative, but you also have to be very well organised."

Having felt he could learn all he could at the restaurant, he took a job in a hotel in the nearby town of Placencia, where he learned how to cater for large numbers of customers. At a restaurant in Salamanca, which he visited to learn more about different types of cooking, he met Julio Reoyo, the chef who ran El Chapín de la Reina, a Michelin-star restaurant in Madrid. He liked José's enthusiasm and offered him a job. José didn't have to think twice. The opportunity to go to Madrid and discover new techniques was too good to turn down. After a year and a half, José rose to become head chef at a new restaurant Reoyo had opened. However, he found himself getting restless. When he mentioned this to a friend of his flatmate's, she suggested he move to London. Within a month, he had packed his bags and was on a flight to Gatwick. He wondered aloud whether travel is in his genes, because many of those who sailed to conquer the Americas came from Extremadura, including his namesake Francisco Pizarro, who took Peru as his prize.

What amazed him most about London was the variety of restaurants he came across. It was in a different league from Madrid. He took a job at Gaudi, a Spanish restaurant in Clerkenwell serving Spain's new cuisine, where he was quickly made sous-chef. But, despite the quality of food being produced at Gaudi, he found that London was not ready for these more innovative dishes. "People didn't know how to enjoy proper *jamón*, proper *chorizo*. If you don't know the Spanish flavours, how are you going to enjoy a foam made with lentils? I realised that if you wanted to get ahead in this city, you had to go back to the Spanish roots – back to simplicity, back to quality, back to flavour."

A spell at Eyre Brothers, a tapas bar in Shoreditch, followed. After two years, he was invited by Monika Linton of Brindisa, who supplied food to the restaurant, to join her in her new restaurant by Borough Market. It opened in 2004 and was a huge success from the outset, soon spawning two other restaurants in Soho and South Kensington, and José started to make a name for himself as a hot Spanish chef.

Yet he wasn't content to work for someone else and, in 2011, he opened José, serving tapas. He had intended to buy larger premises in Bermondsey Street, but the deal fell through, because someone else stumped up more money at the last minute. "Brindisa was good for me, I was good for Brindisa. But it was time to move on. I came to London with 300 euros – I don't have much more now. I bought shares in Brindisa and sold them back to the company. With that money I was able to open José. And it was busy, busy, busy from the first day." Pizarro is not a tapas bar but a restaurant, he declared. "You can have a starter or a main course to share."

His third restaurant, José Pizarro, which opened in Broadgate Circle in 2015, is more geared towards tapas. "When I opened in Broadgate I already had quite a lot of followers in the area. Many people criticised me for going to the City. The *Daily Telegraph* asked why this guy was going to cook for City boys. 'City people don't have a clue. All they care about is money.' I'm sorry. City boys and girls are very clever, they don't throw away their money, and they know what they want. I can do business wherever I want. It's not up to a newspaper to tell me."

He now employs eighty staff. Although he has no problem finding chefs, it's not so easy finding front of house staff, he admitted. He said he has only really got involved in the business side of things in the last two years. Before that, he was more focussed on PR. He found someone to mentor him in business. "I'm learning a lot, but at the same time I'm a chef. That's my main thing." Because he doesn't have any investors or a business partner, he is free to develop the restaurant any way he wants. "As you know, when things are going well, you have to work even harder. What I do is a job because it's how I make my living, but it's also a passion."

TV chefs who open restaurants are often criticised for never being there. So how much time does he spend in the kitchen? "I still cook. I'm usually in the kitchen in Pizarro and José Pizarro each week", he said. "I get ideas everywhere. When I was in Abu Dhabi, we went to a Lebanese restaurant and they cooked liver with pomegranate. I had never thought to put pomegranate with liver. I might put this in my next book or put it on the menu here. Food is amazing. You are always learning."

Like most chefs, he maintains that the most important thing in a restaurant is consistency. "I tell my chefs, 'Don't try to be clever; be consistent.' If you want to open a tapas bar, don't do good food one day and bad food another day. You don't have to go to a Michelin-star restaurant in London to eat good food."

So what is the essence of Spanish cuisine? "It's all about the ingredients. As you know, the Mediterranean cuisine is all about the olive oil, it's about the freshness, and it's about flavour."

"But I guess you could say that about Italian food", I suggested, as a burly, bearded chef came into the restaurant to begin his shift and was greeted with pats on the back by the other staff.

"Absolutely. It's the same thing. I was cooking chicken breast and pumpkin in olive oil with rosemary and a sauce in Abu Dhabi this week. There weren't many Italians cooking there. Two or three people came up to me and said, 'I don't know what you do, but when you are on the stage the whole tent smells amazing.'"

While there are many similarities between the food in the different regions of Spain, he said there are also clear differences. "Spain is a country with seventeen countries in it. We are really regional and local. *Chorizo* is *chorizo*, but the recipe from my mum will be different from the recipe from someone next door. One of them might use more *pimentón* or something. The most important thing with a Spanish restaurant is the quality. Quality, quality, quality."

When I asked him if he thinks we might see Spanish restaurants in London marketing themselves by regional food, he said it would be a good idea, but added with a grin, "I don't think I could open an Extremaduran restaurant yet. Extremadura's not very well known at the moment."

If someone Spanish is going to open a restaurant in London, they need to understand the market, he insisted. "It's very competitive in London. Just because you do well in Spain doesn't mean you are going to do well here." And they shouldn't come into one of his restaurants and try to poach his staff, something that has happened before and is a practice he strongly disapproves of.

Opening a restaurant is a dream that many of us interested in food secretly have. Because we enjoy cooking and entertaining at home, we figure that, maybe, we could do this successfully in a high street. We see ourselves at the end of the evening having a glass of wine with grateful customers and lapping up their praise. So what is José's advice?

"So many people say to me, 'I have money and I want to open a restaurant.' I always tell them to be around very good people. Have a good chef, a good manager. If you want to open a restaurant to entertain your friends, don't open it. A restaurant is a business where you can do well or you can lose a lot of money. Zucca, an Italian restaurant next door, is very good but it's going to close. They can't make money because the rent is too high … Restaurants are a difficult business. It's a business where you have to be there all day. You have huge overheads. If you close the restaurant for ten days you still have to pay rent, you have to pay electricity, you have to pay staff … But if you are doing fine, it's a lovely business. The thing I love really is people. It's why I love this job. I meet people I never thought I would meet. I never thought I would go to the Houses of Parliament or go to Number Ten."

His visit to Number Ten to meet the Prime Minister, David Cameron, occurred when he was invited by the Sustainable Restaurant Association to join 150 other influential figures in the British restaurant and food industry, to celebrate the success of the industry and the key role it plays in attracting tourists and businesses to Britain.

Running just three restaurants means he can use his flat nearby as his office. "I bought it a few years ago. Prices around here are crazy now. Crazy! I wouldn't be able to afford to buy it today."

Despite all the success and accolades in London, he is still passionately attached to Extremadura. He talked with great affection about the Royal Monastery of Santa María in Guadalupe, a place important to Spaniards because of its association with the reconquest of Spain by the Catholic Kings and the arrival of Christopher Columbus in the Americas. "Guadalupe is the most beautiful place ever. When I was small, I used to go there with my dad and when you are in the square you see the church and this incredible view."

Perhaps more than in any other country, food and religion are often entwined in Spain, something that goes back to the way the Church enforced its rules about fasting in Lent and on other days when meat was forbidden. Monasteries controlled much of the food at one time, in many areas. The monks made cheese, grew vegetables, farmed cattle and sheep, and made wine and brandy. Nuns, too, produced food, and some became known for their baking and pastries. As Claudia Roden writes in *The Food of Spain: A Celebration*, "The peasants who worked the vast Church lands gave over to them much of their produce in lieu of rent and maintained the monasteries' vegetable and herb gardens. In the south of Spain, when monasteries took over Moorish palaces, the monks turned the interior patios into herb gardens." This connection between religion and food survives today at Guadalupe. The monks run a restaurant for the pilgrims, who come in great numbers each year, and José loves to eat there when he is back in Extremadura. "It's traditional Spanish food."

The monastery also has an important link to one of the most popular ingredients in Spanish food. "As you know, the Catholics were the ones who had the money and they ate like kings. *Pimentón* came from the monastery at Guadalupe. The Spanish *conquistadores* brought them as a gift for King Ferdinand and Queen Isabella, who passed them to the monastery to cultivate."

Pimentón de la Vera is smoked and made solely in the valley of La Vera, about an hour's drive from his family home. The *pimentón* is made in smokehouses that line the pepper fields in La Vera. In autumn, the peppers are hung from rafters and smoked over fires of holm oak before being ground to a fine powder.

For José, London has become the centre of the culinary world. "At one time, London was looking at what was happening in New York. Now New York is looking at what's happening in London. Yet some Spanish people still think food in London and the UK is very bad. It's not. There are bad places but, at the same time, if you go to Barcelona and you eat in Las Ramblas, it's shit! You can have bad experiences anywhere."

He can envisage more Spanish restaurants opening around the UK, but reckons it will be slow progress. If the right opportunity came up, he would consider launching a restaurant outside the capital. He hasn't ruled out opening a fourth restaurant in London, he admitted. If he does, it will be a different concept. "If you do the same thing, you get bored. You always have to do something new to keep people interested."

"If you open a fourth restaurant you might have a problem", I joked.

He's used up José, Pizarro, and José Pizarro.

"No, no!" he broke into a broad grin. "I would use my mum's name, Isabel."

What he would like to do in the next few years is open a small farm hotel in the Extremaduran countryside, so that people from Britain can experience a part of Spain they might be unfamiliar with. And they could also try one of his favourite cheeses, Torta del Cassar, made near Cáceres, which was intended to be a hard cheese but, because of an error in the production, ended up soft. If he achieves his dream, and I'm sure he will, then it will tie up his life and career as a chef very neatly. The boy who didn't want to work on his father's farm and ended up a top chef in London marks his success by returning home and setting up a farm.

José insisted that, whatever success he has had or will have in the future, for him, it will always be about the food. "My friend, when people recognise me on the street, it's nice but it's not what is driving me to do more things. If people have a good experience here in the restaurant, it's something that will stay with them. That is lovely."

11. The Michelin Star

"Food doesn't need to be boring. And I want to show this on the plate. I want the customers to see that the chefs behind the plate are having fun and are proud of what they are doing."

Sergi Sanz, Ametsa with Arzak Instruction

I was never sure what to think of what is sometimes called "molecular gastronomy". I'd read about how Spanish chefs such as Juan Mari Arzak and Ferran Adrià were supposed to have turned cooking upside down by using test tubes, syringes, foams, and "deconstructions", and even serving dishes on computer screens. It all sounded gimmicky, as if it might be something designed to provide dinner party conversation pieces for people eager for something new in the culinary world. The late Santi Santamaria, a top Catalan chef and a critic of molecular gastronomy, had once remarked, "We chefs are a bunch of fakes who work to entertain snobs and make ourselves a fortune." I wondered if he was right. Was this new Spanish cuisine nothing more than a version of the emperor's new clothes? Or was there something really important behind it? Were Arzak and Adrià taking gullible people for a ride, like Tracey Emin did with her unmade bed when it was exhibited at the Tate Gallery? Or were they, as some insisted, sheer geniuses?

I was in the kitchen at Ametsa with Arzak Instruction, the restaurant of The Halkin hotel in Belgravia, an area of central London whose elegant, white stucco streets house many of the capital's embassies and consulates. In such an exclusive area, it comes as no surprise that the forty-one-room Halkin boasts five stars. A young bearded chef leaned over a white plate and slowly brushed it with stripes of green plankton, doing it with all the skill and concentration of an artist, seemingly oblivious to the constant clatter of pots and pans and sizzling going on around him. Leaning closer, he then added three V-shapes and briefly admired his work before carefully spooning two plump scallops on to the plate and placing it on a tray. A runner in a pale blue shirt and black trousers stood watching silently, almost reverently, poised to take another tray up the stairs to the restaurant for the lunchtime diners.

Ametsa with Arzak Instruction is an odd name for a restaurant, as some newspaper food critics were quick to point out when it opened its doors in 2013. It sounds like something has got badly lost in translation. If there were awards for the most badly named restaurants, then this would surely win it. It's a real mouthful and one that I struggled to remember when I told Bea that I had lined up an interview with a Michelin-star chef. In the end, I just called it Ametsa.

Nevertheless, Ametsa with Arzak Instruction was the first Spanish restaurant in London to win a Michelin star, awarded in 2014, and today it's one of only two in the capital that hold one of the coveted stars. The entry in the 2016 *Michelin Guide* for London says of Ametsa, "There is a wonderful vitality to the cooking and, whilst the techniques are clever and the presentation striking, the dishes are very easy to eat and always able to satisfy."

The man responsible for Ametsa's entry into the restaurant super league is thirty-seven-year old executive chef Sergi Sanz. When I arrived at The Halkin, I must admit that I had low expectations of the interview with Sergi, because the PR company I'd had to go through to arrange it had informed me that one of their team would be waiting to meet me in reception. It's hard to get a good interview with someone when you have a PR person sitting there like an umpire at a tennis match. There was a time when it would be unusual for restaurants and hotels to employ PR companies. The fact that many now do illustrates how slick and sophisticated sections of the food business have become. But the PR woman disappeared with a wave when the affable Sergi came to meet me and invited me to come down to the basement to see the kitchen.

The restaurant's odd name signifies that Ametsa is really an outpost of the three-Michelin-star Arzak restaurant in San Sebastián, the coastal city on the Basque country coast famous for its gastronomy. Ametsa is a partnership between Arzak and The Halkin's owner, Como Hotels and Resorts, which operates a dozen luxury hotels around the world. Prior to Ametsa taking up residence, The Halkin hosted Nahm, a Thai restaurant run by Australian chef David Thompson, which also received a Michelin star. In fact, there's still a wok in the kitchen.

Juan Mari Arzak is regarded as one of the founders of what has come to be known as "nouvelle Spanish cuisine". In the mid-1970s, inspired by the nouvelle cuisine of France, Arzak began playing around with traditional Basque dishes in his San Sebastián restaurant and went on to win three Michelin stars. He now runs it with his daughter Elena, voted best female chef in the world in 2012.

So here I was, watching Sergi, his name embroidered on his white chef's jacket, and his team of chefs in action. The kitchen was in full swing, as it was midday: customers were arriving in the restaurant upstairs and the bar, where tapas is served, was open for business. Another runner appeared at the bottom of the stairs and nervously handed Sergi a ticket. Sergi glanced quickly at it and called out above the hum of the air conditioning, "Table Two! Two more set menus finishing. One hake and one pork." A young female chef carrying a tray of dehydrated black olives squeezed apologetically past me. Another chef opened a plastic container, scooped out some red powder before sprinkling it on a wooden board, then carefully slid on a piece of hake followed by a seaweed dressing of vinegar, olive oil, and chilli peppers. Someone else was busy shelling a tray of langoustines. The kitchen uses between sixteen and twenty kilos of them a week, all caught off the coast of Scotland. After the shell, roe, and innards have been removed, a wooden skewer is inserted through each langoustine so that it doesn't curl up. The day before, the kitchen nearly ran out of them because of a problem with the supplier.

Sergi doesn't like a lot of shouting in the kitchen, preferring to create a calm atmosphere. This is something, I suspect, that reflects his own character. He comes across as modest, disciplined, proud of the kind of food he is creating, and studious. He's about as different in temperament from Gordon Ramsay as you could imagine.

If you've ever been into a busy kitchen in a restaurant, then what hits you immediately is how well organised it is. Without this, it would be impossible to keep that constant flow of dishes coming to the restaurant every few minutes. Sergi reckons that Ametsa is the fastest restaurant in London when it comes to the time between placing an order and it arriving on a table.

I noticed, pinned to the wall, a list of current voucher schemes. It includes *Time Out* and the *Evening Standard*. In such a competitive market as London, even Michelin-star restaurants have to offer discounts to get people through their doors. Sergi, however, sees this as a way to introduce the restaurant to people who might not think of coming to it.

Sergi might be a Michelin-star chef, but he doesn't think he is above doing some of the more menial tasks that must be carried out in a kitchen, such as standing by a sink and filleting a mountain of pork knuckle. "I like to run the pass and service and I like to be the first in the kitchen and the last leaving. I want to keep control. It's not because I don't trust the staff. I take days off and holidays. This project is still at the beginning. It's a baby. It's only three years old and I need to be at the front. In two years' time I can still manage this and start another project", he said.

The pork knuckle will eventually be slow cooked and find its way on to the menu as "muddied pork terrine", garnished with small greens and edible flowers, and served with a thick pork jus reduction spooned on top.

"We are not a traditional restaurant and we don't cook in a traditional way", Sergi insisted, leading me over to a white circular piece of equipment that dehydrates ingredients. He lifted up the lids of its different sections to reveal parsley leaves, sunflowers, pieces of melon, and rocket, as well as bread soaked in vegetable stock.

The menu at Ametsa is unlike anything I've encountered before. It includes foie corn cob, which is foie gras terrine stuffed inside the corn – replacing the cob – and served with popped corn; Ibérico ham on a bread pillow; squid in black ink stuffed with the diced tentacles, garlic, onions, and peppers and cooked in the traditional Basque way; and cold tomato-strawberry soup served in a shot glass. The clove custard, toasted milk, and pineapple ice cream is a big favourite with the customers. Sergi showed me a dish of mussels, which were not really mussels but something else, which I can't remember, and green tomatoes, which were not really green tomatoes, but were made with potatoes. Noticing my expression, he smiled and said, "We use a lot of fakes and illusions."

I wondered aloud if he had done anything experimental with *padrón* peppers, one of my favourite Spanish dishes, and the easiest and quickest one to cook. All you do is toss them around in olive oil and sea salt for a couple of minutes. Not yet, he said, but he might do. He uses a different kind of pepper, *guindilla*, which is long and thin and comes from the Basque country.

One of the most popular dishes at Ametsa is suckling pig, which, he said, is the signature dish of the restaurant. "People love it and ask if it is Spanish. Why would it need to be Spanish? We are in Britain. The pig comes from Yorkshire."

Apart from a set menu and an à la carte menu, Ametsa offers a nine-course tasting menu, which consists of small portions of dishes, similar to tapas. It includes three starters, fish, meat, and desserts. The idea behind a tasting menu is to give customers a wider experience of the food. But, Sergi acknowledged, at £105 (or £154 with five glasses of paired wine), it's not cheap.

He talked about "playing with textures and flavours", telling me that pieces of quinoa, a type of grain, which are served at breakfast are cooked in the oven, dried, and then deep fried.

None of this sounded like the Spanish food I thought I knew. So what actually makes a recipe Spanish? "It's Spanish because I'm Spanish, my way of cooking is Spanish, and it's the ingredients. You need to use Spanish produce and cook it in a Spanish way. You can take a simple potato and cook it in many ways. But if you mix it with eggs and onions and pan fry it, it will become a *tortilla*. You have the basics of Spanish cuisine and you develop it."

When I asked what he thinks the essence of Spanish cuisine is compared to French or Italian, he thought for a moment. "Wow! That's such a complicated question. Spanish cuisine is not just about tapas. It has a lot of variety. It comes from the different regions of Spain, which are very rich. Food is very important in Spain. Every meeting, or every party, is always around a table or a bar." He paused and added, "Spanish food is more rustic."

For chefs, being awarded a Michelin star is the equivalent of winning a medal in the Olympics. The stars are awarded after anonymous visits by mysterious figures known as Michelin inspectors, who never make themselves known and always pay their own bill at the end of the meal.

A tyre company giving out awards for good dining is not as odd as it might seem. The Michelin guides began in 1900 when tyre manufacturers André Michelin and his brother Édouard came up with an idea to boost the demand for cars in France. They produced a free book containing useful information for motorists, including maps, instructions for repairing and changing tyres, and lists of car mechanics, petrol stations, and hotels. Guides to other countries soon followed. The brothers then recruited a team of inspectors to review restaurants and, in 1926, the guide began awarding a star to places considered exceptional. By 1936, they had created the famous three-star system. One star means "A very good restaurant in its category", two, "Excellent cooking, worth a detour", and three, "Exceptional cuisine, worth a special journey."

If you want to know just how important Michelin stars are to chefs, then you only have to read Marco Pierre White's *Devil in the Kitchen*, his riveting account of his obsession with achieving three Michelin stars. He eventually achieved his dream, at his restaurant in Wandsworth, but later handed the stars back, feeling disillusioned and that he had gone as far as he could go in the culinary world. More recently, the obsession with achieving Michelin stars was also depicted in the film, *Burnt*, in which Bradley Cooper plays a chef who, having won a battle with drugs and alcohol that destroyed his career in a top Paris restaurant, comes to London determined to win back the three Michelin stars he once held.

Sergi is aware that restaurants can get their stars taken away by Michelin, which can lead not only to a drop in business but also to a devastating blow to a chef's pride. In 2003, French chef Bernard Loiseau, said to be the inspiration for the character of Auguste Gusteau, the celebrity chef in the film *Ratatouille*, committed suicide after speculation grew that Michelin was about to pull his restaurant's third star.

"If I lose a star, I'll kill myself", he allegedly said.

Ametsa looked unlikely to win a Michelin star when it opened in 2013. Several critics who visited it were unimpressed both by the restaurant and some of the food. Zoe Williams in the *Daily Telegraph* wrote, "Taste-wise, the broth was too salty, you couldn't discern much else, and the squid in the parcels was cut up very small, which, given its toughness, reminded me of gravel. Mine was also soupy, with a great cloud of crunchy, pale-yellow noodles; it looked like one of those 'directional' cushions Ikea always has on 'special'." However, she wasn't totally negative, adding, "But the prawns were excellent, cooked with utter precision, fresh and delicate. And the corn soup was intense and smooth."

Sergi heard the news about the Michelin star when he was working in the kitchen with the breakfast chef. "The general manager came in and said something, but I didn't understand him because he seemed really nervous. He then grabbed me and gave me a hug. I didn't know why he did this and asked him to repeat what he had said. I then stopped what I was doing and called over the breakfast chef, and then I cried a bit. I went outside for a cigarette and to text my parents. When the other chefs started to arrive, I told them we had won a Michelin star and said that it wouldn't change anything. We would just carry on doing what we were doing."

Juan Mari and Elena Arzak must have been jumping for joy back in San Sebastián when news of the Michelin star came through. Ametsa is their first restaurant outside Spain. The star also confirmed that they had made the right choice in putting Sergi in charge of their mission in London.

"It's an achievement", said Sergi. "It's like a prize you receive after hard work. To be honest, I never dreamed of winning a Michelin star."

It was tough when the restaurant first opened, he confided. I asked him how those spiky reviews in the early days affected him. Did he take it personally? "Not at all. The critics didn't know me. They didn't know who was in the kitchen. I needed to hear what they were saying and learn from it."

In those early days, he admitted, he got some things wrong, such as portion sizes. "We started with small portions, because plating up small portions rather than large portions looks nicer. But in Britain, in this kind of restaurant, people expect larger portions. And there was a vegetable dish we had on the menu as a vegetarian option that wasn't popular. I could never find the proper vegetables. I tried it with chard and artichokes, but at the end of the day we removed it because people didn't like it."

Sergi could have ended up in a very different career. After he left school in Barcelona, he was intending to be an engineer. His parents encouraged him to study engineering at university, as they thought it would provide a secure future for him.

"When I finished my degree, I decided it was not for me. I needed something else to make me feel fulfilled. Then I started thinking, why not try working in a kitchen? I was always passionate about cooking and watched chefs on TV programmes and bought books. I also prepared food for many friends' parties and I was always the person in charge of the table."

But Juan Mari Arzak was only the prophet of the new Spanish cuisine. The messiah appeared in the form of Ferran Adrià. One day, Sergi was checking the web site of elBulli, Adrià's famous restaurant in Catalonia, when he spotted a vacancy. He applied and was offered a job at Adrià's two Michelin-star restaurant in Seville. "My CV was almost empty because I had no experience. I didn't expect to hear back But they phoned me and asked me if I was still interested."

Not having had formal culinary training wasn't a barrier to joining

Adrià's enterprise. Despite his reputation, Adrià hadn't been through a culinary college, but had started out as a pot washer. Sergi didn't have to do this. He was taken on as a commis chef, the first level of the chef hierarchy.

Although he didn't get to know Adrià well, he would see him when he came to the restaurant to say hello to the staff. It must have been like the pope visiting. "At that moment, he was regarded as one of the best chefs in the world. It was around the time of the *New York Times* article. His way of thinking is different to the common way of thinking. Most chefs would think of something normal. He thinks of one more step and he questions everything. That's his genius. I felt very proud being very close to him. He was my boss and he was my idol."

After absorbing some of Adrià's ideas and techniques, Sergi felt it was time to move on and joined the team at the Michelin-star Drolma restaurant in Barcelona's five-star Majestic Hotel, run by another top Catalan chef, Fermí Puig. When that closed in 2011 because of the economic problems in Spain, he joined Puig at his new venture, Petit Comité, a more modest restaurant, by all accounts. "Before, in Drolma, I was officiating as a bishop in a cathedral. Now I am a small parish rector, but happy", Puig quipped in an interview at the time.

Following his spell with Puig, Sergi was appointed executive sous-chef at the luxury Hotel Villa Magna in Madrid, which boasted three kitchens. While there, he wrote to Juan Mari and Elena Arzak, asking if he could come and observe how they did things. His thirst for knowledge must have impressed them, because they agreed. "I was just watching and taking notes. I wanted to develop, to keep learning, to feel as comfortable in a three-star kitchen as I do in my house."

Sergi got on well with the Arzaks and, when they agreed with Como Hotels and Resorts to take on the restaurant at The Halkin, they offered him the position of executive chef. Sergi was looking for a new challenge and says he saw the opportunity to run an exciting new project in London as destiny. Although he had never been in charge of a kitchen, he knew what would be expected of him. To ensure that he fully understood the Arzak way of doing things, he spent six months working in the kitchen with them before catching the plane to London.

The Arzaks visit Ametsa two or three times a year and Sergi regularly travels to San Sebastián to discuss ideas for new dishes with them and to learn new techniques. This will sometimes involve spending time in their laboratory, which contains over 1,500 ingredients, all neatly labelled in plastic containers. "The Arzak family need to agree with the dishes I want to put on the menu here, but normally they are happy. They have never punished me because I put something on the menu they didn't know or which wasn't right."

Sergi has created his own laboratory in the walk-in fridge, where he experiments with ingredients. When he is developing a new recipe, he has to carry out a lot of tastings before he finds the right flavours and textures. "It takes a minimum of two months from when I first get the idea to coming up with the final dish. There's a lot of work after the first idea to develop it. Sometimes you need to leave a dish you're trying to create for a couple of weeks and then come back to it. It's a process. When you get an idea you need to question it. The first idea might be good but it also could be better."

Finding the right combination of ingredients is more about experience and intuition than science, he maintained. "I had never worked with horseradish before coming to London. I mixed it with cheese and discovered it worked."

Eating shouldn't just be about eating but also about fun, he thinks. For example, when customers order the monkfish, the waiter puts the plate down on the table in front of them and scatters dried peppers over the fish. That's why the dish is called monkfish confetti. "Food doesn't need to be boring. And I want to show this on the plate. I want the customers to see that the chefs behind the plate are having fun and are proud of what they are doing."

Does he think there are similarities between a chef and an artist? "At the end of the day, cooking is art. If you are an artist, you need to do art and to do art is to do something different, to be able to produce emotions in people. A painter will create emotions with his paint; a chef will create emotions with his plate. You want to create an experience for the people who eat your food. It's not just the food. It's the staff, the ambience, everything."

Of course, the dishes he creates are only as good as the team of chefs who work with him. Although he's employed French, British, Latin American, and Romanian chefs, he prefers to work with Spaniards, because he thinks they better understand the kind of dishes he wants to create. Following the departure of a pastry chef for Italy the day before, all his chefs are now Spanish. He also likes to move chefs around the different sections of the kitchen – breakfast, room service, pastry, larder, fish, and meat – so they become competent in different areas.

Prospective chefs are always given a try out in the kitchen. "I don't want to talk about position, salary, or shifts at the beginning. I want them to understand what we are, what we are trying to do, and what we want."

He thinks the glamour associated with TV chefs can lead to some young chefs having unrealistic expectations when they begin work in a kitchen. However, he soon knows at Ametsa who can handle the pressure and long hours. His chefs often work ten to twelve hours a day, and sometimes fourteen on Saturdays.

I gained an insight into just how tough it is in a professional kitchen when I worked as an occasional kitchen porter and pot washer at a three-star hotel in my teens. I can remember the heat, the noise, chefs tearing around as orders arrived, and blazing arguments between the head chef and the head waiter, a bossy Italian. As a kitchen porter, I had to do all the grimy and unpopular jobs, such as scrubbing heavy pots and pans, emptying and cleaning the walk-in then putting everything back in, and heaving heavy black bags of waste through the back door to the bin area outside. When I finished a shift, I was soaking wet and every one of my muscles ached. I couldn't imagine why anyone would want to be a kitchen porter for any length of time.

I was surprised when Sergi told me that he sometimes watches cooking clips on YouTube when he's at home. I thought it was only amateur cooks, like me, who did this. "There are some very good ones. When I start, I cannot stop." He's a fan of Heston Blumenthal and Jason Atherton. When I asked him if he's ever watched any clips of Rick Stein's journey through Spain, he shook his head and scribbled his name down on a piece of paper.

Working in a hotel kitchen and working in a restaurant kitchen are very different, he explained. Chefs need to feel part of the hotel and mix with the staff in the other parts of it. Despite the restaurant being in a hotel, Ametsa has regular customers. He showed me a list of room service orders and says he knows many of the names and what they like. He tries to find time during the service to go upstairs and talk to the customers. "I love it when they want to come downstairs to the kitchen."

So what does he find most rewarding in being a chef? "There are two things: the team and what they learn and how they develop. This is very important to me. The second is the guests." He told me that three chefs from Texas recently visited the restaurant and then came to speak to him afterwards. They told him that they had been in another very good restaurant in London but the food wasn't as good as they had eaten at Ametsa. "I felt very important", he says with genuine modesty.

164

Although he knows some of the other Spanish chefs in London, he says he's isolated. "I spend almost the whole day here in the kitchen. With our shift patterns, it's not easy for chefs to meet each other. From time to time I might meet other Spanish chefs at big events or at the Spanish Embassy."

He doesn't have the energy he once had and confessed that some of his chefs are quicker at doing some tasks than he is. He used to cycle and go hill climbing, but no longer has the time to do this. His bike is at the hotel, but he hasn't ridden it for a while because of pains in his leg.

He doesn't consider the four years he spent at university studying engineering a waste. "From engineering, I learned how to plan a restaurant and how to plan a dish. You have to be organised as a chef."

One day, he would like to be his own boss and maybe run several restaurants, although he has no desire to own his own place, unless he could find the right kind of business partner. In the meantime, he is focussed on maintaining the high standards he has set at Ametsa. "I think getting a second Michelin star is the way for me to keep the first one", he said reflectively.

I left Ametsa feeling humbled by Sergi's generosity in allowing me to spend time in the kitchen with him. I wasn't sure that I really grasped the idea of food being art, which I think is how Sergi sees it, but I could see why Ferran Adrià and Juan Mari Arzak were regarded by some people in the same way that others might regard Rembrandt or Monet. Perhaps, though, Sergi is right and chefs are, or at least could be, artists.

Not long after I had interviewed Sergi, the *Sunday Times* published its list of the best 100 restaurants in Britain, and Ametsa made it on to the list for the first time. "The cooking is expressive, full of vivid colour, contrasting textures, and both visual and verbal puns", said the entry.

On a Friday evening a few weeks later, I unexpectedly found myself sitting in Ametsa with Bea. She had booked a table as a birthday surprise. Usually, when I go to a restaurant, I'm anticipating the food. This time I felt anxious. My anxiety was due to the fact that I was about to eat my first ever meal in a Michelin-star restaurant, and I wasn't sure what the protocol was. The prospect of sitting in a really posh restaurant felt intimidating. When I mentioned this to Bea, she laughed and said, "I feel like I'm going to the theatre."

With its white walls, wooden floor, and white tablecloths, Ametsa looks rather plain, even clinical, until you look up at the ceiling. Around 7,000 golden test tubes filled with spices are suspended from it, intended both to resemble a wave and to highlight that the food is from the Basque country, famous for its fish and seafood, and is also part of the new Spanish cuisine.

I had never eaten in a restaurant with a tasting menu before, so I suggested to Bea that one of us had it, and one of us the à la carte, so we could share. When I told the waiter, he furrowed his brow. "Ah, that might not be a good idea, as we tell customers to allow two and a half hours for the tasting menu."

"Oh", I said, surprised at both the length of time the meal would last and the waiter's confidence in being able to predict it.

"If you have the à la carte and the tasting menu, one of you might be sitting for a long time without anything to eat", he said in his best diplomatic voice.

So we took his advice and opted for the tasting menu. I decided to have the paired glasses of wine, curious to see how this worked. With a tasting menu, you choose the fish and meat dishes from the à la carte menu. I opted for suckling pig on carob crumbs and John Dory with crispy beetroot sauce; Bea went for tuna with cinnamon, deciding not to have a meat dish, as she might feel too full.

Act one began with the "*aperitivos*": small pieces of scorpion fish attached to a metal stand; "onion rock" with marinated anchovies; mango *chistorra*, which looked like dark brown crisps; and ham with filo pastry served in tiny test tubes. Each dish was visually stunning and the combination of flavours and textures was amazing.

When act two, the "*entrantes*", began, Bea and I were licking our lips in anticipation, and we weren't disappointed. Having seen the scallop and plankton dish prepared in the kitchen when I interviewed Sergi, I now got to try it. "It's meant to look like the bottom of the sea", the waiter explained. Bea looked wide-eyed and said it looked too good to eat. When I tasted the soft scallops and crispy plankton they were absolutely delicious. Langoustines on a bed of lichens and a "runny graffiti egg" with green sauce followed.

"This isn't just about eating, is it?" I said to Bea. "It's about using the senses – the taste, touch, what it looks like, the smells, everything."

"Yes, and I can see the psychology in it. It's about surprising people", she replied. "You wonder what's coming next."

I totally agreed. When I told a young waiter that we had never eaten food like this, he smiled knowingly and said, like a kindly ticket collector on a train, "There's still a long journey to go." What had become clear to me was that the waiters were part of the show, not just incidental players, which is what Sergi had meant when speaking about the food being fun.

The waiter then appeared with the John Dory accompanied by small balls of beetroot and a beetroot vinaigrette. "This … is the spherification", he announced solemnly, lowering his voice, as if he was introducing a very special guest.

Spherification is one of the sacred mysteries associated with the new Spanish cuisine. As Ferran Adrià demonstrated in that YouTube clip, it works by spooning a liquid such as, in this case, a purée of beetroot, into a solution of alginate, a natural gelling agent found in seaweed. The liquid then forms a sphere, turning hard on the outside but keeping the liquid on the inside. The aim is to give the diner a surprise.

I thought the idea was clever, but not as clever as Bea's tuna with cinnamon. This arrived under a domed glass. When the waiter lifted it up, the aroma from a burning cinnamon stick perfumed the air, like incense in a church.

"Wow!" she said. "But where does cinnamon fit in to Basque food?"

"I've no idea", I said. I would have associated cinnamon with the Moorish influences found in southern Spain. Nevertheless, although the dish was visually impressive, this time we both felt that the combination of flavours didn't work that well.

My suckling pig was a different story. It was sensational. Both the meat and the crispy skin just melted in my mouth.

When the third act began, I had begun to feel that I was taking part in a sort of culinary Olympics. I could tell that Bea was beginning to wonder whether she would be able to eat any more. She looked relieved when the next dish turned out to be a shot glass of homemade *sangria*. When I took a sip, it sounded as if a firework display was going off in my mouth, or that it was being pelted by hailstones.

"That's popping candy", said the waiter, clearly enjoying my startled reaction. "It cleans the palate."

The grand finale was a light-as-a-feather orange French toast with spinach followed by a chocolate truffle. Then came another theatrical moment. As the waiter poured a sauce on the truffle, it slowly collapsed before our eyes. We looked at each other and shook our heads in amazement.

"I can appreciate the scientific side", said Bea. "It's a very clever combination of different elements: the ingredients, the flavours, the textures. It's like chemistry! You see how one element reacts with another."

But, throughout the meal, there was something else happening. I felt that the wine was taking a fantastic journey around the regions of Spain. It began in Andalusia with a glass of Amontillado Gran Barquero sherry from the Montilla-Moriles region, which had a wonderful cream and chocolate flavour that lingered on my tongue. Next, we travelled up to Catalonia (white), then across to Castilla y León (white) and on up to La Rioja (white) and Galicia (red). Our journey ended over on the east of Spain in Murcia (red) after returning to Andalusia for a delicious sweet wine from Malaga.

I awoke the following morning, my mind filled with memories of the food we had eaten, the theatricality of it all, and that wine tour around Spain. Yes, it was expensive, and not everyone could afford to dine at Ametsa. Yet there are special occasions when some of us might pay a similar price for a ticket to a concert or a show we desperately want to see. What's the difference? I once spent a huge amount when I took my daughter to see Celine Dion perform at the O2 Arena in North Greenwich. And it was worth every penny. The important thing to understand about Ametsa is that it's not just about eating delicious food; it's also about entertainment. What Sergi knows is that food isn't just something we eat. It's like a good film or song. It works on our senses to transport us briefly to somewhere else, which is where many of us often want to go. And Ametsa had done just that.

12. The Celebrity Restaurant

"Sometimes it's the small, subtle things that determine whether you are in a Spanish restaurant."

Abel Lusa, Cambio de Tercio

If you want an illustration of just how far Spanish cuisine has come in London, then head to Old Brompton Road, which meanders from South Kensington to Earls Court, through the red brick Victorian mansions and white stucco streets that are so typical of this prosperous and swanky area of west London. In a section at the Earls Court end you will find Cambio de Tercio. You might not have heard of it, but plenty of royalty and showbiz stars have.

I was impressed by José Pizarro having two restaurants in the same street. But Abel Lusa has gone one better. A couple of doors along from Cambio de Tercio, a traditional restaurant, is Capote y Toros, specialising in *jamón* and sherry, while across the road Tendido Cero serves tapas. A short distance away in Parsons Green, Abel runs a fourth restaurant, Tendido Cuatro, London's only restaurant dedicated to *paella*. You can even phone up for a take-away.

I caught up with him early one afternoon in Cambio de Tercio's gin and tonic bar, which offers an astonishing choice of eighty gins from around the world. The mustard yellow, bright red, and pink walls are decorated with modern paintings of bullfighters. In one, a matador and a woman with pointed breasts sit opposite each other. Several hundred bottles of wine from virtually every region of Spain were stacked along one of the walls, behind glass. Slim, and dressed in an open-neck blue shirt, Abel bears a passing resemblance to Roger Federer, which is appropriate, as he is a tennis fanatic. With four restaurants to run, life is always busy, but it had become even more hectic since his wife gave birth to their second son the week before.

It's unusual having three restaurants in one street, I suggested when we sat down. "Yes, yes, but not just in one street, because it could be a very long street. Our restaurants are close together. For us, it's a great success. Old Brompton Road is a very affluent area. People dine out quite a few times a week. I've always said that if you have a good idea for a restaurant it has to be in the right neighbourhood. In this area, for example, if we had a lot of students, we couldn't serve what we do", Abel replied.

Cambio de Tercio gets so busy some evenings that seventeen waiters will be scuttling between tables. Yet Abel claimed he never tells people he is fully booked when they phone up. "Even if we are, we will always give you an option. It might be a crazy option. We might say we can give you a table at eleven o'clock, and you might say no. But I hate going out to places and finding them fully booked. Yes, you are fully booked, but it's ten o'clock. I'm sure you're going to have tables free in the next half an hour. But they tell you they are fully booked because most of the owners don't work there or the staff don't care enough."

The menu includes slow-cooked red mullet with caramelised cauliflower, nameko mushrooms and mullet jus; grilled lamb cutlets with lamb sweetbreads, black garlic purée, and baby artichokes; and mini burgers made from wagyu beef, said to be the world's most expensive variety.

"Our food reflects food from around Spain but not necessarily traditional recipes", said Abel. "We use Spanish ingredients and local ingredients. We don't describe a dish, for example, as cod from a Bilbao recipe. We create dishes. Our *patatas bravas* are cooked differently. We scoop out the middle of the potato and put the sauce in it. And we cook suckling pig in a traditional Spanish way but the sauce and garnish are different."

If customers want food made with good ingredients, then that is going to cost them, he emphasised. "Good Spanish restaurants shouldn't be frightened of charging high prices for the best ham in the world. Before, if you opened a tapas bar, it had to be cheap. That was the image of tapas. If you sell cheap, then you have to buy frozen prawns and the cheapest *chorizo*. You have to be second best. Whatever you need to charge, you charge, and then it's up to the people to judge if they want to come."

I didn't mention to Abel that I was once one of those people who, when looking for a restaurant, would always opt for the menu that was cheapest. It was only when I started cooking more seriously at home that I realised that, if you wanted better ingredients, then they were going to cost a bit more. That's not to say that some restaurants don't take customers for a ride. Recently, I checked out the menu of a restaurant trading under the name of a famous TV chef and was astonished to see that it charged thirty-five pounds for fish and chips. I think this is outrageous for what is a comparatively cheap dish to cook. Yet, presumably, some people are prepared to pay it.

For many of Abel's customers, I would imagine that money isn't a problem. When he reels off the names of some of them, it's as if he's reading from an edition of *Hello!* magazine. They include everyone from Kate Middleton and Prince William to Hugh Grant and Jeremy Clarkson, along with Premier League footballers – Stamford Bridge is a short distance away. And, when they are in town, Robert De Niro and Dustin Hoffman like to pop in. Despite such a glitzy clientele, Abel says he doesn't have a problem with paparazzi turning up. And if they do, then it's usually because one of his diners wants their photo in the papers.

Some celebrities have become Abel's friends. Ian Botham attended his wedding and Kylie Minogue, who lives nearby, often pops in for a coffee and a catch-up. Among the dozens of smiling faces in the photos on his Facebook page, one crops up more than any other: Rafael Nadal.

"I have a personal friendship with Rafa and I travel to many tournaments with him and his uncle and the team", said Abel.

So how often has he been to the restaurant?

"About sixty or seventy times. He first came here when he was sixteen and played at Wimbledon for the first time."

Nadal is a big fan of seafood and fish and, when he comes to Cambio de Tercio, he will often order the octopus or wild turbot.

I couldn't resist asking if Federer ever came to the restaurant.

"No, he doesn't go out much. But Djokovic used to come at one time. A friend of mine who is the PR person for Rafa used to do his PR as well."

Apart from tennis, Abel is also a keen fan of bullfighting, which is why the name of each of his four restaurants refers to its terminology. Cambio de Tercio, for example, refers to the third change of direction of a bull's charge, while Tendido Cuatro refers to the fourth section of seats in a bull ring.

Cambio de Tercio opened in 1995, when Spanish cuisine in London was still trying to make a name for itself among diners, and especially among those prepared to pay well for a good meal. Its reputation has not gone unnoticed in Spain. King Juan Carlos has eaten there, and, in 2003, Abel and his business partner David Rivero were awarded the Premios Alimentos de España by the Spanish government for being the best Spanish restaurant outside Spain.

It's no wonder that Abel sees himself as a pioneer of good Spanish cuisine in London. "When I first opened, I wasn't serving modern Spanish food, like we do today. It reflected what was being cooked in Spain back in those days. Spain back then was not an exciting country for gastronomy. It has always used good ingredients and provided good traditional food, but it wasn't a leading country in terms of gastronomy, as it is today. When we opened this restaurant, we couldn't be as innovative as we have been for the last ten years."

In those days, he claimed, Spanish restaurants in London tended to be run by Spaniards who had no previous experience in catering and hospitality. Often, they opened a restaurant as an alternative to working in the construction industry.

"The people who came here from Spain forty or fifty years ago and opened restaurants were the brave ones – more than the people who have opened restaurants in London in the last few years. Now, it's easy. Spain has exploded in the world of gastronomy. Out of the fifty best restaurants in the world, you have three or four Spaniards in the top ten. Ferran Adrià at elBulli has influenced every top chef in the world, from America, to Noma in Copenhagen. To open a Spanish restaurant is simple, but to make it a destination is very hard."

Abel grew up in La Rioja, where, unsurprisingly, one of the things he learned very young was the importance of wine. As a child, he was taken to visit wineries, where he saw the grapes growing and learned about how wine was made. In September, his parents often took him to friends' vineyards to help with the harvest. "We would sometimes spend the weekend there and have barbecued lamb chops", he recalled with affection.

At the age of fourteen, he went off to catering school and spent the next five years learning about cooking and hotel management. "I heard about a new catering school that had opened in a nearby village and my school took us to see it. My older cousin was studying there, and I saw her peeling an orange with a knife and fork, like it used to be done then. I thought to myself, if this is studying, then this is what I want to do. It doesn't seem to be very hard. As soon as I went there, I liked it, and, according to the professors, I was good. I was taught how to set a long table, how to open bottles of wine, and how to make cocktails. It was great fun. I didn't think about what kind of future I might have. I just thought of my studies and that one day I might end up working in a restaurant."

During his time at catering school he discovered that he was more interested in how restaurants were run, and meeting customers, than standing over a stove in the kitchen. After completing the course, he worked for three years in a two Michelin-star restaurant in Madrid. "I learned about good manners and how customers should be treated."

The owner of the restaurant was friends with the owners of Albero y Grana, an upmarket Spanish restaurant in Sloane Avenue, and he arranged for Abel to be interviewed for a position as a waiter there. Abel flew out to London, got the job and, within a year, was promoted to maître d'.

"It was very modern, very posh, and extremely expensive, and it was always packed", he said. "It was a grand place with rich clients and good-looking girls. It put Spanish gastronomy on the map in London.

Albero y Grana was run by a Spanish woman and her Malaysian husband, who was a director of Emporio Armani for Europe. A Malaysian company pumped lots of money into it, bringing over a Michelin-star chef from Madrid and an interior designer from Barcelona.

Yet not everyone was appreciative of the decor, I discovered. When a reviewer from the *Independent* had visited the restaurant she was taken aback by the deep red walls and the ashtrays containing sand imported from Seville, which, she guessed, were meant to evoke bullfighting. "In fact, I have never seen a restaurant in Spain indulge in such dramatics – not in Seville, not in San Sebastián, not in Barcelona, not in Burgos, not in Madrid. But in London, a Spanish restaurant can more or less make itself up as it goes along."

It was during the two years Abel spent working at Albero y Grana that he first got the idea to open his own restaurant. An Iranian customer, who was in the property business, was so impressed by the way he treated the customers and his enthusiasm that he suggested he open his own place.

Even though Abel was only twenty-five years old and had been in London only two years, he and David Rivero, whom he had first met at catering school, scraped together enough money to open Cambio de Tercio, buying second-hand kitchen equipment and serving simple meals and tapas. Abel thought that the idea of having three areas – for the bar, for tapas, and for the restaurant – worked at Albero y Grana, and decided he would model his restaurant the same way.

When I suggested that the Old Brompton Road was a very expensive place in which to open a restaurant, even back then, he shrugged, "But London is getting to a point where there are no cheap areas. Here, Soho, Covent Garden, it's pretty much the same. There's no cheap rents any more."

Abel could have looked for premises in a less expensive area, but he wanted to attract the same type of clientele as Albero y Grana. And you would be less likely to do that if you were located in a back street of Hammersmith or Shepherd's Bush.

Although he took his inspiration from Albero y Grana, and even hired one of its chefs to run the kitchen, he said he didn't try to recreate their dishes. He replaced the chef a few months later with a female chef from San Sebastián, who he felt was better able to cook the kind of food customers would like.

"If Albero y Grana had been in Camden or Shoreditch, or one of those younger areas, I would have tried to recreate that", he said. "But I ended up in Sloane Avenue, one of the poshest streets in London, and my restaurants are in the same area. So I tried to learn what the English liked when I worked at Albero. When I first opened we used some of the same suppliers. We didn't try to recreate the dishes, but the way of doing things."

It wasn't long before companies approached him to suggest taking out adverts in magazines, promising they would increase his customers. He wasn't taken in by their spiel, especially given the amounts of money they were asking. He knew the best PR was offering customers not just good food and service but also a free *pacharán* (liqueur) or brandy at the end of an evening. Hiring out the downstairs area for parties also helped him both to generate extra income and to build a profile for the restaurant.

"I remember the first review we had from Fay Maschler in the *Evening Standard*", said Abel. "She loved the food. What she wrote reflected the passion she saw on those plates."

Matthew Norman in the *Daily Telegraph* also raved about Cambio de Tercio and described it as a refuge for Rafael Nadal when he's in London. "If I were world number one, which seems a long shot, the thought of this restaurant would see me throw the first-round match 3-6, 1-6, 0-6 to the world number 479 from Papua New Guinea, and leap into a cab to the Old Brompton Road before the sun set on the opening day."

Delighted by Cambio de Tercio's success, Abel was quick to spot another opportunity. He realised that some of his customers just came for tapas, not a full meal. So in 2003 he opened Tendido Cero, across the road. In 2010, he completed his hat trick of restaurants on Old Brompton Road when he opened a *jamón* and sherry bar, Capote y Toros.

"Although there are several other places in London selling sherry, in terms of diversity, we have the second largest sherry bar in the world after a tiny place in Tokyo", he claimed. "We stock 120 labels. Not even in Spain would you find a place that comes anywhere near us. Most Spanish restaurants would sell ten or fifteen kinds of sherry at the most. We also serve tapas in the sherry bar and we use sherry in cooking, either by marinating – as an ingredient – or as a vinaigrette. This is a great novelty."

From the outset, Abel has worked hard to build up a wine list that reflects many of the different regions of Spain, including the lesser known Alella, south of Barcelona, which has just six producers; Dominio de Valdepusa, near Toledo in Castilla-La Mancha; and Somontano, near the Pyrenees in Aragon. Customers have over 500 wines to choose from, with prices ranging from £20 to a whopping £2,400. "We showcase the best Spanish wines. Most of them you won't find anywhere else in London. We have become a destination for people who love Spanish wine."

The standard of Spanish cuisine in London is, with a few exceptions, excellent, Abel maintains. "One thing is to promote Spanish tapas restaurants, but another thing is to promote great Spanish ingredients, wine, and service."

He's not a fan of chains, concluding that, because they are controlled by investment companies, everything comes down to making money and cutting costs. "When you are a chain you can't guarantee good service. If we went for lunch to one today and then came back a year later, most likely all the staff will have gone." Another problem with chains offering the cuisine of a particular country, he said, is that what they serve the customers is not always authentic. "Mexicans always complain that nearly every restaurant outside Mexico is a Tex Mex. That food doesn't exist in Mexico."

Having staff with the right attitude is crucial to success, he insisted. "I have great staff and, in a business like this, you have to look after them as well as you can, money-wise and in other ways. There's nothing more rewarding for a client to come in and be recognised by seven members of staff. 'How are you?' 'How are you?' Then your mood is going to be different when you sit down. You are going to enjoy it even if we just give you a piece of bread."

So how does he get staff to share his vision of what a restaurant should be? "Our staff have to be fast, they have to be smiley, and they have to be skilful", he said. "The ambience in the evening is very nice, with the music and noise."

Running his own business means he has flexibility, especially when it comes to his family. He drops his two-year old son off at the nursery in the mornings and usually starts work in his office at midday, making a point of having lunch with the staff. "I'm lucky that I can give more time to my children than most people working in the city."

Abel loves the buzz of the restaurant business. That's why, most evenings, he's at the door of Cambio de Tercio to greet customers. To do well in the business, he stressed, you have to have a passion for it. "Catering in general is a different business to many others. If you don't like it, it can be a miserable life. It will be clear in your eyes when you serve customers. How many miserable waiters do we see? But if you like the business, it's fantastic. You meet new people all the time and every day is an experience. You enjoy seeing people enjoying themselves. They say, 'Thank you very much for a wonderful evening.' Sometimes you might have a drunk person who is very funny. You will always have something to come back home and tell your wife about. You aren't sitting in front of a computer all day."

He invited me down to the kitchen, where chefs dressed in black were busy preparing for the evening crowd. A large vat containing beef stock was bubbling away and trays of fried chicken were coming out of the oven for the staff lunch.

I wondered what the white table in the middle was for. "Is that for the staff?" I asked.

"No, it's for customers who want to see the action", he replied. "Some people like to see their food being cooked. So they can have their meal here."

Eight years ago, the kitchen and the back of the restaurant were destroyed when a fire broke out. Yet Abel was up and running in a month, deciding not to wait for the insurance company's decision.

Again, I wanted to know what it is, exactly, that makes a dish Spanish. What did Abel think? "We have to be realistic sometimes. A fillet of beef, lamb cutlets, sweetbreads, artichokes, garlic: every country in the world uses them. If you had a dish of lamb in a blind tasting, you might not know if you were in a Spanish restaurant, an Italian, or a French one. If we give a French chef garlic, artichokes, and lamb cutlets and ask him to cook it, and say the same to a Spanish chef, the flavour at the end will be completely different. Sometimes it's the small, subtle things that determine whether you are in a Spanish restaurant. Italians and Spanish have similar ingredients but each will cook them differently. I'm not saying we are better or we are this or that. But we do different things."

13. Taking on the Italians

"Every other gastropub is now using either Serrano ham or olive oil. Before, you wouldn't find olive oil in a gastropub."

Ben Garcia, Products From Spain

I always thought that I had a fairly good knowledge of London. Bea says you can drop me down anywhere in it and I can find my way around. It's true. I might not have a clue how to fix a dripping tap at home, but I have an inbuilt sat nav to get me around London. I put this down to my childhood, when I would spend hours in my bedroom staring at maps, and the fact that I'm a member of that exclusive club of men who have never owned a car.

However, in the thirty years I'd lived in London, I'd never been to Park Royal. I knew it was in the west, somewhere between edgy Harlesden and gritty Acton, but that was about it. Now, I had a reason to go, because Park Royal is where you will find the oldest Spanish wholesaler in London, Products From Spain.

When you travel around London and see all those steel and glass office blocks everywhere, and companies involved in financial services, digital technology, or marketing, you could be forgiven for thinking that there was no one left who did jobs that demand hard graft and getting your hands dirty. So, when you arrive at Park Royal, you feel that you've been let into one of the capital's big secrets. How could I live in London for so long and not know about such an important part of the city? Hemmed in by railway lines and sidings in the north and the Western Avenue funnelling traffic in the south are business units, warehouses, offices, and yards. They seem to go on forever. The only respite from this bleak but strangely fascinating landscape is the Grand Union Canal, which sneaks through the middle of it. If the West End is London's playground, then Park Royal is its workshop. Everything from Guinness to Heinz soup, Routemaster buses, and Arden's cosmetics has been produced here over the years. Those companies have since gone, but McVitie's is still here, turning out its famous digestive biscuits and Jaffa Cakes, and in recent years Carphone Warehouse has moved in.

With 2,000 companies – most of them small to medium size – employing an estimated 30,000 workers, Park Royal is said to be the largest industrial estate in Europe. Wandering around it, you find companies making lights, cleaning laundry, processing metal, repairing cars, and producing mannequins for shops. And there are around 500 companies involved in food. There's a chance that the sushi roll, sandwich, ready meal, or orange juice you purchased in the high street was produced in a unit at Park Royal and delivered in one of the hundreds of anonymous white vans that whizz up and down its network of service roads each day.

Products From Spain occupies two units at Park Royal. I don't know why, but such an industrial setting seems odd for a company selling Spanish food. As its sales manager Ben Garcia explained, it's been here for twenty-five years, having begun in a shop on Charlotte Street in the West End back in the 1950s, supplying not just the Spanish but also the Portuguese community. Today, Products From Spain employs seven staff and supplies restaurants, hotels, delis, coffee shops, and gastropubs. Over the last fifteen years, it has seen a major increase in orders as a result of the number of Spanish restaurants opening.

"All our products are selling well at the moment. We can't complain", said Ben, a quietly spoken, affable man with a salt and pepper moustache. "Spanish products are becoming more popular. A lot of

English people go to Spain and they know more about Spanish food than they used to. For example, English people will now ask for Serrano ham when they go to a deli. A few years ago they would have asked for Parma ham. Spanish food is almost at the Italian level in Britain."

On shelves in a small room, some of the company's 450 products were displayed, along with stacks of *paella* pans and tapas dishes. The most popular products, said Ben, are Manchego cheese, Serrano ham, cooking *chorizo*, extra virgin olive oil, and tinned fish and seafood from Galicia.

"Every other gastropub is now using either Serrano ham or olive oil", said Ben. "Before, you wouldn't find olive oil in a gastropub. If they are using Italian olive oil, you might be able to persuade them to use Spanish olive oil if you offer a better quality and a better price."

One of Products From Spain's two delivery vans goes out every day, making around twenty or thirty drops inside the M25. "We deliver by area. For example, today it might be the West End and south, tomorrow West End and east, the next day south-east, and then north-west. We can deliver to every single one of our customers each week."

Ben spends part of his week visiting customers, making sure the existing ones are happy and trying to win new ones. He doesn't come across as one of those pushy salesmen. His manner seems more like that of a helpful receptionist in a hotel. He maintains that the success of Products From Spain all comes down to the price and quality of the products. He grew up in a small village in Galicia and came to London when he was fifteen, settling in Kensal Rise, which was then home to a small Spanish community. Before joining Products From Spain twenty-seven years ago, he started out as a mechanic and then went to work for another importer of Spanish food.

Being surrounded by Spanish produce all day, it's perhaps not surprising that he rarely eats out in Spanish restaurants. Yet he stills loves the food of his homeland, especially *chorizo*. "My favourite Spanish dish is anything with *chorizo* in it. I love it! I could eat *chorizo* every single day for breakfast, lunch, and supper. But probably I'm a bit of a maniac when it comes to *chorizo*."

How did he think Spanish food would develop in the future? Could all of this interest just be a trend that would eventually fizzle out? "No. It will become even more popular. In about fifteen years, I think Spanish food in Britain will be level with Italian. We will catch them up."

Leaving Products From Spain, I reflected on Ben's prediction. I agreed with him that the popularity of Spanish food in London is not a passing fad. But will it overtake Italian, as he suggests? Accurate statistics for restaurants listed by ethnic cuisine are hard to come by. One report I read put the number of Italian restaurants in the UK at over 5,000. Even though they have been around for over a hundred years, that sounds very high. Let's say London has 1,000 Italian restaurants. If this is reasonably accurate, then it's way ahead of my estimate of around 200 Spanish restaurants and bars.

Given this, Ben's prediction looks unlikely to come true, especially as Italian chains such as Jamie's, Ask, and Carluccio's are continuing to expand and independent sourdough pizza places seem to be opening everywhere. Pizza and pasta are popular the world over in a way that Spanish dishes aren't, and I can't see that changing. The sole Spanish chain, La Tasca, closed many of its forty restaurants in 2015 after being bought by another company. I'm not sure what to read into this, as La Tasca seems to have had a troubled history and hasn't always received universal acclaim for the kind of Spanish food it serves. One restaurant owner I met even went as far as to say that it has damaged the reputation of Spanish cuisine.

At the time of writing, David Muñoz, whose Madrid restaurant has three Michelin stars, is planning to open StreetXO in Mayfair. With his mohawk hair and pierced ears, he has the look of a punk rocker. The *New York Times* described him as "Spain's new culinary enfant terrible". The international director of the Michelin guides went as far as to compare him to Ferran Adrià. Apparently, chefs at his London restaurant will cook with woks and flames in full view of diners, serving up what Muñoz calls Spanish street food with south Asian influences.

Whether this kind of fusion will characterise the Spanish cuisine of the future is debatable. But it raises that question again: what makes food Spanish? Is it the ingredients, the chef, or the style of cooking? While *chorizo* might be unique to Spanish cooking, ingredients such as potatoes, onions, beef, and prawns are found in other cuisines. As for the style of cooking, again you can see similarities with other cuisines, especially Italian and French. What's more, not all chefs working in Spanish restaurants are actually Spanish. I know a tapas bar where the owner is English, the chef Hungarian, and the front of house staff French and Polish. Is that really a Spanish restaurant? Do you have to be Italian to cook a pizza, or Indian to cook a curry?

If there's one component of Spanish cooking that Spaniards love more than anything else, apart from ham, then it's olive oil. With over 300 million olive trees, Spain produces more olive oil than any other country, comfortably ahead of its nearest rivals, Italy and Greece.

The first time I learned about olive oil was when I was a student in the early 1980s and spent a month working as a volunteer at a care home in the Suffolk countryside. It was in one of those gorgeous villages with thatched cottages, a quaint pub overlooking a duck pond, and an ancient parish church. It was like stepping back into an idyllic England of the 1950s. My job was to help the gardener look after the grounds, where potatoes and other vegetables, as well as lots of weeds, grew. It was hard work, but enjoyable, because of the sunshine and a lively bunch of other students who were also volunteering. It was one of those golden summers you remember years later with fondness and nostalgia. After work, we played football on the village green, went for long walks along the narrow lanes, and spent evenings chatting in the corner of the cosy pub with low wooden beams.

Several of the students were from Barcelona, and I can remember them always insisting proudly that they weren't actually Spanish but Catalan. I hadn't realised that Catalans considered themselves a separate people from the Spanish. One time, I asked one of the girls what kind of food she missed from back home.

"Olive oil", she said dreamily.

"Olive oil?" I'd only ever heard olive oil mentioned in the Bible.

"Oh, I love olive oil!" she said, adding that for breakfast, she rubbed bread with tomatoes and then drizzled olive oil and salt over it.

I found this very strange. I assumed olive oil was just like the vegetable oil my mum used when she cooked chips. I couldn't imagine putting that on a piece of bread and then eating it. I know now that *pan con tomate* is a classic, yet incredibly simple, dish found not just in Catalonia but also in other parts of Spain.

These days, when I'm about to cook, one of the first things I take out of the kitchen cupboard is a bottle of olive oil. However, when I look at the bottles on the supermarket shelves I end up scratching my head. There are so many to choose from: olive oil, extra virgin, virgin, light, mild, pure. Which one should you use when you cook? When you watch someone like Jamie Oliver or Antonio Carluccio cooking on TV, they often say, "Put in a splash of good olive oil", but never explain which particular kind.

So when I was wandering along the market stalls in Bromley one Saturday afternoon and came across one selling bottles of extra virgin olive oil and jars of green olives, I thought I might find some answers. I discovered that the stall was run by Mar Fernandez-Garcia, originally from Malaga but now living in Blackheath with her English husband. At one time, Mar worked in banking. Now she is on a mission to introduce more people to Spanish extra virgin olive oil. She had set up a web site and, a few weeks before, at Mas Q Menos, a Spanish restaurant in Wardour Street, had held an olive oil tasting for members of the Spanish Olive Oil Club, which she established through the social network group Meet Up.

Not long after, Mar emailed me with an invitation to an olive oil tasting session one evening at Bar Tozino, the *jamón* bar in Bermondsey. I joined a group of eight foodies around a long table outside, where a red canopy had been erected in case it rained. One of the group looked familiar, but I couldn't place him. Then the woman sitting next to me, who was also an importer of Spanish extra virgin olive oil, when she wasn't working as a guide in country houses, mentioned that this man had been a finalist in BBC1's *MasterChef* competition. I realised that I had seen his photo in the food section of the *Guardian* web site. When I got talking to him I learned that, since the programme, he had done very well, cooking food for people in their homes, doing cookery demonstrations, and running seminars on how to set up supper clubs.

Mar began the tasting by explaining how olive oil was produced. When she first visited an olive oil producer, she said, she had a romantic idea of an old mill with the paste being pressed with stones. Instead it turned out to be more like a modern factory. I learned that once olives have been harvested, using either the traditional method of beating the branches of the trees with a stick, or a large machine on wheels that operates a little bit like a combine harvester, they are washed, filtered to remove any twigs or stones, then crushed. This leaves a thick paste from which the olive juice is extracted by separating the oil from the vegetable water and solids before it is transferred to steel containers, where it is filtered and stored until bottling.

The extra virgin olive oils Mar imports come from Andalusia, which accounts for around seventy-five per cent of Spain's olive oil. Andalusia's Minister of Agriculture, Fishing and Rural Development, Carmen Ortiz, predicted a substantial increase in olive production for the 2015-2016 harvest season. She said national production of olive oil could reach 1.2 million metric tonnes, a forty-three per cent rise over last year's output of just above 800,000 tonnes.

According to Mar, there are only three categories of olive oil to be concerned with: olive oil, virgin olive oil, and extra virgin olive oil. "Even some Spanish people often don't know the differences between extra virgin olive oil and the others", she claimed. "In England you can't buy virgin olive oil, but in Spain we have lots. I haven't seen it anywhere here."

The differences between the types of olive oils are not to do with the olives used but with the production process. The best olive oil is extra virgin, because this is pure oil from the olives. Nothing else is added. It contains a lower level of oleic acid than other olive oil varieties and more of the natural vitamins and minerals found in olives. As the flavour of oils from different olives varies, some are better suited to particular dishes, she explained. "For example, we could choose Arbequina, which has a light and fruity taste, for a dessert or to bake a cake. Hojiblanca and Picudo are good for salads, and fish or meat marinade, and Picual, which is intense and fruity, is good for stews or roasts. For dipping with bread you can use any depending on how adventurous you are."

Mar, becoming more and more evangelical, then instructed us to close our eyes. "Now pinch your nose and open your hands." I wondered what was going on, but did as she asked, feeling slightly silly. She moved around the table and I felt some powder being placed on my palm. If anyone walks past, I thought, they might think we are some kind of weird religious cult. "Smell it and say what you think it is", she instructed. The smell was familiar, but I couldn't work out exactly what it was. Cinnamon, someone said. He was right. This was a way of getting us to exercise our powers of smell. Next, she invited us to pick up off the table one of the small blue glasses containing extra virgin olive oil, sniff it, and then taste it. I lifted the glass and thought I could detect an aroma of tomatoes or grass. The taste seemed slightly bitter. Mar then told us to take a sip of water from another glass and a slice of apple. "This is to clean your palette."

We tasted three more types. The second seemed milder and the third more peppery. "This is what I think of when I think of olive oil", said the guy from *MasterChef*, licking his lips after tasting the fourth type.

Mar's eyes widened. "It's from the supermarket! It's very cheap."

"Oh", he murmured, looking surprised. This oil was meant to be the joker in the pack, as far as Mar was concerned. She was trying to show how the brands she imports from Spain are superior to some of the cheaper ones you might buy in your local supermarket. But I had to agree with the *MasterChef* guy. I too thought the fourth one tasted pretty good. It wasn't too bitter and had a pleasant flavour.

"What's the best way to use olive oil when you are cooking?" I asked Mar afterwards.

"The common use for extra virgin olive oil is dressing salads or raw vegetables. We also use extra virgin olive oil in braising, like *sofrito*, which consists of garlic, onion, peppers, and tomatoes cooked in olive oil, and is a base for many dishes from all over Spain such as stew, *paellas*, fish, or vegetables."

Olive oil can be used for frying, she explained, but it is important not to exceed 180 degrees Celsius in the frying pan. "When deep frying, the olive oil forms a crust on the surface that impedes the penetration of oil and improves its flavour. Fry small portions to avoid a rapid decrease of the oil's temperature and let the food stand afterwards on absorbent paper to remove excess oil."

Even though Mar had been cooking with extra virgin olive oil for many years, it wasn't until she was diagnosed with type 2 diabetes that she started to become interested in it. "It was after having my second son, Oscar. I had put on a lot of weight. It's the kind of diabetes you get when you are older and because you aren't eating properly or getting enough exercise. The doctor said to me that the first thing he was going to do was put me on a Mediterranean diet and the only fat it would include would be extra virgin olive oil. He told me not to use butter."

The doctor also suggested she ate the kind of food cooked by Karlos Arguiñano Urkiola, a Spanish chef and popular TV presenter whose catchphrase is "Tasty, tasty and with nutritional value." Olive oil is widely regarded as having health benefits. Because it contains mono-unsaturated fats, it can help lower your level of cholesterol and reduce the risk of heart disease.

Mar started to read about olive oil, of which there are around 260 varieties or brands, and became more and more fascinated by it. "I was learning English at an adult centre in Lewisham and I had to do a short presentation as part of my assessment. So I decided to talk about Spanish extra virgin olive oil. I spoke about its health benefits and food pairing."

She has been on a number of courses to learn about olive oil, including one at the University of Jaén in Andalusia, run by the International Olive Council, an intergovernmental organisation based in Madrid and made up of the members of the European Union plus a number of other countries, including Israel, Morocco, and Uruguay.

Olives are quite fragile, she told me. "If they are damaged they ferment and produce a bad taste and a bad smell. This would not be considered extra virgin olive oil. The soil, the weather, insects, and harvesting all affect the flavour of olive oil. Olives are green and later they become black. When they are green they have more health benefits. They produce anti-oxidants." Unlike wine, extra virgin olive oil doesn't get better with age, she went on. It's the other way around. The fresher the olives, the better. Furthermore, olive oil should be kept in a cupboard in the kitchen, away from heat and light.

Competitions to find the best olive oil are held in Spain each year. There's even one called The International Award for Cooking with Extra Virgin Olive Oil, with £8,500 in prize money. At Madrid Fusion in 2015, nearly sixty competitors from Spain, Italy, Greece, and Portugal battled it out, with Xanty Elías of Restaurante Acánthum in Huelva winning top spot for his olive oil toast with crispy croaker (fish) skin, featuring Oro Bailen and Cortijo La Torre olive oils.

"Taste the oil from a tree under which Caesar may have taken his *siesta* on any given day during his Spanish campaign – that's a message that makes a major splash in a New York City restaurant", remarked an official from the Spanish Association of Municipalities of the Olive Tree, at its 2013 award ceremony for spreading the culture of olive oil.

Olive oil is a multi-million-pound business and its production in Europe is governed by strict rules. Yet where there is big money to be made, there is nearly always corruption. And in the world of olive oil there is an ongoing battle to tackle those who try to deceive customers with their products. Italy is also famous for its olive oil, of course. However, the chances are that the Italian olive oil you buy in the supermarket actually comes from Spain. It's just been bottled in Italy and had a label stuck on it.

Mar appeared in the Channel 4 TV series *Food Unwrapped* to talk about fraud in the olive oil industry in the UK, the fifth biggest importer of Spanish olive oil. The programme chose, at random, six extra virgin olive oils (Spanish, Italian, and Palestinian) sold in British supermarkets. After carrying out tests, it claimed that while all six passed the chemical criteria, three failed when it came to the sensory criteria. In other words, they didn't smell like extra virgin olive oil should do. The manufacturers dismissed the findings because a panel of experts approved by the International Olive Council didn't carry them out.

Whatever the truth of the TV investigation, there is clearly deception going on with some olive oil producers. For example, in 2008, more than 400 police officers in Italy conducted an investigation dubbed "Operation Golden Oil", which led to the arrest of twenty-three people and the confiscation of eighty-five farms. In his book *Extra Virginity: The Sublime and Scandalous World of Olive Oil*, Tom Mueller explained just how lucrative olive oil is. "Olive oil has historically been one of the most frequently adulterated products in the European Union, whose profits, one EU anti-fraud investigator told me, have at times been 'comparable to cocaine trafficking, with none of the risks.'"

14. Streets of London

"If I go into a restaurant to sell Spanish ham, I don't want to feel embarrassed. I want to be able to say, we have the best products, and you are going to try them and tell me that I'm right."

Esther

While sitting outside my local café in south-east London one cloudy afternoon, making notes about this book, my attention was caught by a young woman standing near the late night shop. She was going up to passers-by and offering them bottles of something. It looked an odd sight. When I heard her say, "It's extra virgin olive oil", I thought to myself, I wonder if it's Spanish? As I watched her, an image came to my mind of a café in Malaga and an old man in a faded white T-shirt pulling an octopus from a blue plastic bucket. What, though, was someone doing selling Spanish olive oil on a street in suburban London, I wondered. Curious, I drank up, paid my bill, and went to speak to her.

I learned that her name was Esther and she worked for a new company in the north of England that was importing what it marketed as luxury Spanish food products. She had come to meet a businessman who had taken delivery of £3,000-worth of extra virgin olive oil from the company. He had said that he was going to store it in one of his shops and then sell it to bakeries. The deal seemed to be that the profit would be split and that he would provide Esther's company with a list of some of his clients. Esther had been concerned when he hadn't produced the client list as promised, and, when he arrived in his van, she discovered that the olive oil hadn't yet been unloaded and that the labels were dirty from yeast and flour. So she had unloaded all the boxes, ignoring the man's protests, and piled them on the pavement. Now she was waiting for her boss to send someone to collect them and, in the mean time, thought she would try and sell the oil to locals.

"I don't know when the van is coming", she said with an air of good natured resignation "Well, this is life. What can we do about it?" I was impressed by her stoic attitude. She seemed to take this unexpected turn of events in her stride.

When I told her I was writing a book about Spanish food, and had just been making notes about it in the café, she smiled and said, "So something good has come out of this."

Pulling out a copy of the company's brochure from her bag, she explained the different kinds of extra virgin olive oil it sold and pointed out the awards several of them had won. She also highlighted some of the other products listed, including jars of queen olives stuffed with garlic and jars of pastes containing olives mixed with goat's cheese, seaweed, and even curry.

Esther had a degree in tourism and an MBA in foreign trade, and had quit her job at the international office of the Spanish government, where she had helped companies export their goods to the UK, to come to London. Her friends told her she was crazy to leave, she said. "They thought British people only liked fish and chips and pies."

However, it wasn't her first time in the capital. Unable to find a job in Spain after leaving university in Zaragoza, she had come here briefly in 2012, living in a hostel and working in, of all places, an Indian restaurant, where she ended up as the manager.

Many Spaniards you meet will insist that Spain produces the best ham, the best cheese, or the best wine. And they will also often inform you that their particular region is better than all the others. Esther was no exception. She came from Teruel in the mountains of Aragon in north-east Spain, where her father's deli sold the town's famous ham, with some of it designated Teruel as opposed to Serrano. She talked excitedly about how she loves *huevos rotos con jamón* (eggs with fried potatoes and ham) and Cabrales cheese, and how her grandmother made the best *paella*, with rabbit, clams, mussels, and pork. In Aragon, she told me, tapas doesn't mean serving portions of food on small plates. Instead it means going to a restaurant and ordering several big plates and sharing them. "We like to eat in Aragon!" she joked.

What led her to London was a desire to introduce more people to Spanish produce, she claimed. "I want to be able to go into a supermarket and see Spanish products and feel proud that I brought them. Some people think Spanish food is only things like *patatas bravas*. I want to bring the real Spanish food."

She stressed that she wouldn't have the same passion if she was selling clothes or shoes. "When I had the interview with my boss, I asked to taste the products the company was selling, because I wasn't prepared to take the job if I didn't like them. I don't like lying to people. If I go into a restaurant to sell Spanish ham, I don't want to feel embarrassed. I want to be able to say, we have the best products, and you are going to try them and tell me that I'm right. This is why we are working with the best producers we have found so far in Spain. We sell the best extra virgin olive oil and the best olives. If I was selling average products, there would be no point in me working for the company."

Trying to persuade Spanish restaurants and delis to buy her products was much harder than she had anticipated, she admitted. So far, she had visited sixty-five establishments and had no success. "When you go into a restaurant for the first time you don't meet the owner. You usually meet a member of staff who will invite you back the following week to meet the supervisor. Then when you meet the supervisor he will say you need to talk to the manager and then the manager will say you need to talk to the purchasing manager. And then after that you might get to speak to the owner."

Her strategy when planning to visit a restaurant or deli was to first check their web site to see what they were selling. With restaurants, she would also analyse the menu to try and work out what seemed the most popular item and what they might need. Her main focus was selling Manchego cheese, *chorizo*, and ham.

Despite this lack of progress, she seemed upbeat, confident that she had a natural instinct for business, like her father who started his deli in Teruel thirty-five years ago. "I'm as stubborn as a mule", she laughed, pleased to have come up with an English phrase. "You can't give up. It's not a sprint; it's a marathon. And it's a marathon that can last a year or more."

I came away after meeting Esther impressed by her tenacity but doubtful that she would make much progress. If a restaurant has built up a good relationship with a supplier, then it's unlikely to switch to someone else, especially a new company, no matter what discounts might be offered.

I kept in touch with her, curious to see how long she could continue knocking on doors. It came as no surprise when I phoned her one day and she told me that she had developed a new approach: selling Spanish gin. Although I had seen Abel Lusa's selection of gin at Cambio de Tercio, I wasn't aware that so many people enjoyed gin. In my mind, I still associated it with the "gin palaces" that existed in London in the nineteenth century and the term "gin and Jag set", once used to describe wealthy businessmen in the Home Counties.

"Gin is very popular in Spain now and there are hundreds of gin clubs", Esther told me. "It's common for some people to have a gin and tonic after a meal. At one time, it was only associated with the over-sixties and, if you had a gin and tonic in a night club, people would wonder why." The gin she was selling was made with eucalyptus and produced in Valencia. "I will often say to a restaurant, 'You have some good dishes on the menu but something is missing.' They will ask which ingredient and I will say Spanish gin. On the drinks menu in some Spanish restaurants you'll see Beefeater gin, not Spanish gin."

Her idea of using gin as an introduction to the other products her company sold appeared to be paying off. When she had emailed restaurants and delis trying to get them interested in Spanish food, hardly any had replied. But when she emailed them about gin it was a different story. A few weeks later when I spoke to her again, however, I discovered that her gin strategy hadn't succeeded, after all. Not prepared to put up with the unrealistic expectations of her boss 200 miles away in a northern industrial town, she had resigned from the company and was now working as a receptionist in a hotel in Waterloo. She told me she was happy and could see an exciting career path in the hospitality industry ahead.

Esther's lack of success in selling Spanish products was nothing to do with her abilities. She was passionate about what she was selling and prepared to lug a heavy bag of samples around the streets of London every day and be rejected. The reason she couldn't persuade restaurants and delis to buy her products is that there are Spanish importers, like Products From Spain and Brindisa, who have been around a long time and have established a good reputation with their customers. If a restaurant is supplied with quality products at a reasonable price, from a company that delivers on time and is trustworthy, why would it take its business to someone with no track record? While there is a growing market for Spanish produce in London, not everyone is going to succeed. To do this, you need not only to have passion, but also to know how to run a business. And you will also need to have done your homework, like Tim Luther when he was planning to open Barrica. From what Esther had told me, her boss hadn't done this. If you haven't worked out how to reach your market, you are doomed to fail.

A sushi restaurant opened near my home last year. On the local community forum, a number of people posted glowing reviews about it. And yet every time I go past, I see lots of empty tables and a waitress staring vacantly out of the window. The problem is simple: it's in the wrong area. If people here go out for a meal locally, then they go to the fantastic Italian trattoria in the high street, the gastropub, or one of the Indian restaurants. Sushi is something people might eat if they went to the West End for a night out.

* * *

I'm standing in the kitchen at home, wearing a black and white striped apron and slicing a *chorizo* on a red chopping board. Tonight, I'm going to cook potatoes with peppers and *chorizo*, a recipe from Omar Allibhoy's book, *Tapas Revolution*. On the work surface, I've assembled a bottle of extra virgin olive oil, a tin of sweet *pimentón*, some tomatoes, and a sprig of thyme, plus garlic cloves, onions, and peppers, what Keith Floyd called the holy trinity of Spanish cooking.

Since watching Rick Stein's TV series about Spain, I have cooked at home nearly every night. Getting married has probably played a part in this. I'm more anchored now. Before, I'd often spend evenings drifting from pub to pub, often eating when I got home late at night. I love cooking now, but when you are single, preparing a meal from scratch can seem too much effort.

Towards the end of my bachelor days, I had virtually stopped buying supermarket ready meals, finding most of them, despite the attractive packaging, pretty bland. When I did cook, it was usually cod and chips, mashed potato topped with Leicester cheese, spaghetti mixed with spoonfuls of Saclà olive and tomato sauce, and mushroom-filled pasta (from Tesco) drizzled with chilli sauce and olive oil. Although I had bought small jars of cumin, coriander, peppercorns, and dried parsley, I didn't have a clue how to use them. Nevertheless, just having them in the kitchen cupboard made me feel sophisticated. I was still into takeaways. I would usually phone for one a couple of nights a week. I ordered so many Margheritas from a local pizza company that they used to send me a Christmas card. I also created "The List", restaurants and takeaways I'd visited and would recommend to other people. But there were no Spanish places on it.

When I first started taking cooking more seriously, some of my efforts in the kitchen were not very good. I lacked knowledge about ingredients and cooking methods. I would sometimes put too much salt in a dish, overcook something, or undercook it. I found a recipe with a long list of ingredients intimidating until I started to break it down into sections: meat or fish, vegetables, herbs, spices, oil, vinegar, and so on. This way, a recipe doesn't look quite so daunting.

Attending cookery classes went a long way to boost my confidence. Seeing a professional chef in action helps to demystify the cooking process. It's like being allowed onto the set of a movie. One of the most enjoyable classes I attended was in a farmhouse in the hills above Sorrento on the Amalfi coast, where I learned to make what the daughter of the family informed me was authentic pizza. It was only topped with tomato sauce, mozzarella, and basil.

Talking to the other home cooks I met made me realise that I was not the only person whose enthusiasm in the kitchen outstripped his knowledge and techniques. I've discovered that cooking, like most things in life, is about practice, patience, and not giving up if you make mistakes. The more you cook, the more confident and competent you get. Now, I might set out to follow a particular recipe and then, halfway through, decide to adapt it. Something else I often do before cooking a meal is watch YouTube clips of proper chefs cooking it. Each will usually cook it in a slightly different way from the other, which means you can pick up valuable short cuts and tips. Not everything I cook turns out brilliantly, though. Sometimes I get a bit carried away and add flavours or ingredients to a recipe that don't work. And I still haven't managed to cook a *tortilla* successfully. Each time I've flipped it over, it's collapsed into a messy goo.

I enjoy cooking because I find it creative, and because it is physical, at least compared to when I'm sitting in front of my Apple Mac. I love the idea of combining different ingredients and trying to produce a tasty dish. When this happens, I have a tremendous feeling of achievement. I'm not just cooking for me, though. I'm cooking for Bea, occasionally Raphael – although he hasn't quite left the chicken nuggets stage yet – and friends who come around for dinner. Cooking a meal is a way of showing love and of providing hospitality. I like nothing more than seeing expressions of delight on the faces around the table when I carry in a dish of something and put it down before them.

I sometimes fantasise about opening a tapas bar in my local high street. With the area changing so much, I could see it being a big hit. I'd have hams and strings of dried peppers hanging from the ceiling, and, on the walls, black and white photos of street scenes in Spain and a map of the different wine regions, with corks identifying major towns and cities.

Yet, having interviewed many restaurant owners, I'm aware how difficult it is to open a restaurant and then turn it into a successful business. It takes between three and five years to do this, I've been told. You have so many overheads, so many things to get right, and so many things that can go wrong. What we as customers don't see when we sit down at a table in a good restaurant is the incredible amount of hard work that has gone on behind the scenes to create that menu, that wonderfully attentive service, and the satisfying food that leaves us saying, as we go out through the door, "I'm definitely coming back here!"

I'm not so foolish as to think that appreciating good food and being a good host at dinner parties at home are reasons to think you would be a good restaurateur. Plenty of chefs and restaurant owners have written about the perils of this. Nevertheless, I still have a yearning to be a restaurant owner.

In typical Keith Floyd style, I take a sip from a glass of red wine from Murcia. I had bought it the day before from the new independent wine shop that recently opened near the station. When I went up to the till, the owner gave me a huge smile.

"Can I take a photo of you?" he asked, picking up his iPhone.

"Er, yes, I suppose", I said, surprised at this unexpected attention.

"Great! You're our first customer."

I liked the idea of being the first customer and also that the first bottle of wine the shop had sold was Spanish.

Bea is sitting on the settee in the living room, helping my son to practise his reading. She is Mexican. "What are you going to cook tonight?" she calls out.

"*Vamos a cocinar patatas a la riojana esta noche*", I say, sticking my head around the door.

"That sounds yummy!" she says. "You know, you're really doing well with your Spanish."

I began learning Spanish a few months ago after signing up to an on-line course, synergyspanish.com. Having failed my French O-level at school, I always thought that I didn't have an aptitude for foreign languages. But the course tries to keep things simple. It doesn't confuse you with too many verb tenses all at once and its lessons are typically ten minutes long.

I'm encouraged by Bea's praise, but I wonder if I will ever be able to speak Spanish well enough to hold a conversation. When we spent a week with her cousin and her Argentinian husband in California, I felt too tongue-tied to try out my Spanish. I thought I'd sound ridiculous. I tell myself that I just need to keep up with the lessons and, gradually, I will reach some level of fluency.

I pour some olive oil into a pan, turn on the gas and, when it starts to heat up, flip in the garlic, onion, and red peppers with a knife. I watch as they begin to gently sizzle and those wonderful aromas fill the kitchen.

Taking another sip of wine, I find myself thinking about that *paella* in a box I had enjoyed so much in my childhood. While wandering along the aisles of my local Sainsbury's the week before, I had searched the shelves for it, curious to see if it was still popular. But it wasn't there. You can buy it on Amazon, I discovered, though. The box looks the same except that the outline of Spain has been replaced by an image of a Flamenco dancer with the word "Seville" written under it.

I tip chopped tomatoes, slices of *chorizo*, and chunks of potatoes into the pan, and stir them around. Then I open the tin of *pimentón* and spoon in the orangey red powder, which always reminds me of the pigment used for making paint. I cook the mixture for a few minutes before pouring in sherry vinegar. For extra flavour, I drop in two sprigs of thyme. I love the scent of different herbs. They remind me of nature. Now I begin to sense that strange magic which happens when you combine the right ingredients. I feel I'm some kind of alchemist. Finally, I add a jug of water, sprinkle salt and pepper, bring the mixture to the boil, and reduce the heat until the pan is simmering gently.

Outside in the garden under a tight, darkening sky, I can feel the

March chill and smell the grass, which is beginning to sprout in thin patches after the bleak winter. I stand on the small patio, looking at the rose bushes climbing up the wooden fence, the plant pots, the lone spindly apple tree, and, beyond, the half-lit back windows of houses. As I hear the muffled sound of another commuter train whooshing past, I inhale the pungent smells of peppers, onions, garlic, and *pimentón* from the kitchen, and I am not in south-east London any longer. I'm sitting outside a café in a village of white houses with orange terracotta roofs set amidst hills carpeted in olive trees. The sun is blazing down from a porcelain blue sky and I can almost taste the heat. In the background, bells from the old church in the square toll solemnly, like they have done for hundreds of years. A smiling waiter in a white shirt glides over to my table, carrying a glass of cold Albariño wine, some crusty bread, and a bowl of plump green olives. But the sound of my son calling, "Daddy!" brings me sharply back to London. I return inside to finish cooking, and to put my passion – and Spain – on a plate.